# *Doing It.*

## *Mind-Blowing Sex Tips You Will Never Forget*

### *(The Fine Art of Intimate Sex)*

# *by* **Angela Sherice**

KARMAIC PUBLISHING

# CONTENTS

# *Doing It!*

## *Mind-Blowing Sex Tips You Will Never Forget (The Fine Art of Intimate Sex)*

By Angela Sherice

Library of Congress Pre Assigned Control Number

LCCN 2010922508

p. cm.

Doing It! Mind-Blowing Sex Tips You Will Never Forget. (The Fine Art of Intimate Sex)/by Angela Sherice.

Sherice.

Doing It! Mind-Blowing Sex Tips You Will Never Forget. (The Fine Art of Intimate Sex)

ISBN 978-09709806-4-9 (KARMAPUB) Angela Sherice

KARMAIC PUBLISHING

UNITED STATES OF AMERICA

Cover art & design by Angela Sherice

Written, edited & proof-read by Angela Sherice

Printed in the U.S.A

***Doing It! Mind-Blowing Sex Tips You Will Never Forget
(The Fine Art of Intimate Sex)*** is a step by step
introduction to understanding of the true meaning of sexual
intimacy and how to use it to add sparks in your own sex
life-to take it to a new level.

Intimate sex is like a fine art: it is the instinctual, mental,
and spiritual behind the emotion and/or physical act of sex-
be it: masturbation, oral-sex or sexual intercourse and its
subcategories.

Like "love," a person can only love to the capacity for
which they know "love." Therefore, they can only give and
receive love to the extent for which they know *how* to give
love and receive that love.

The same is true for sexual intimacy. Sexual intimacy is
often confused and misconstrued because we can all agree
that sex-itself *is* an intimate act, therefore, we
automatically equate "intimacy" with "love." But the fact
is-all people who "love" and all people who are "in love,"
are not necessarily creating sexual intimacy between one
another.

Sexual intimacy is not a given for two people who are
necessarily "in love" any more than the fact that it can
shared between two people who aren't "in love."

Sexual  intimacy is created by merely understanding the
instinctual, mental, and spiritual goings on, behind the act
itself: the spoken and the unspoken-the action and the
reaction-why you do what you do, and how to fully utilize

an entire intimate moment.

***Doing It! Mind-Blowing Sex Tips You Will Never Forget (The Fine Art of Intimate Sex)*** is a practical guide to teach you exactly how to love your lover in ways they have never experienced, and promises to give you mind-blowing sex tips that I guarantee you will never forget.

# ~DEDICATION~

I write this book to you for this reason:

With countless conversations I've had with men and women over the years, I've always wanted to write a book about sex and intimacy-because both are big necessities for us, as human beings, as is our relationship and connection to other human beings.

Over the years and in countless conversations, I've found that true sexual intimacy was rare, if ever, there.

Where sex and intimacy are concerned, I've found that differentiating the two can be confusing for some people, just like differentiating what love from infatuation is-and what love from lust is.

While gathering the thoughts in my head after these conversations; I decided that "sexual intimacy" between people, is a little-bit like "love." A person can only *love* to the capacity for which they *know* "love." Therefore, they can only give and receive love to the extent for which they know *how* to give love and receive that love.

The same is true for sexual intimacy, except that sexual intimacy is confused and misconstrued because we can all agree that sex-itself *is* an intimate act. And we equate "intimacy" with "love." But the fact is that all people who love and are "in love," aren't creating sexual intimacy and sexual intimacy doesn't have to be created amongst two people who are necessarily "in love" either.

Sexual intimacy is created by merely understand the mental, emotional and spiritual goings on, behind the act itself-the spoken and the unspoken-the action and the reaction.

I am a people, nature and animal watcher.

I love nature and human behavior-no matter the subject.

Subjects about sex and all its many subcategories are all one thing to me.

I don't cringe at one and shun the other and judge the third. I never curled my face in ways that

I've seen people do about the taboo and risqué, even when I was younger. Before I could fully understand it, I had always been overly curious about us as sexual beings-and wondered about the things that we do not talk about-and how they are "done-about."

Since early in life, I've always been that "girl's" girl.

That friend of all my girlfriend's friends that whenever there was a question, concern, or issue about: menstruation, sex, boys, and matters of the heart, goals, dreams-you name it; I was *always* the go-to girl.

It was just my "thing"-my role in those departments.

*Generally* speaking, about everything in life, I'm curious about how they work and what makes something work with something else [that brings that something else] into existence and gives it "love" and life.

Sex, and intimacy is something that I've always loved and remain curious about-feeling the need to dissect every aspect of it, from the mental to the spiritual to the physical aspect of; how it is apart of us, how we can connect with it and then create it.

So, as natural as sex and intimacy are to me, I wanted to write my book the very same way.

I did not want to write about "safe" subject matter-dressing up and sugarcoating real and tangible issues and curiosities that I know men and women really have and want other points of view on (outside of the traditional).

Sex and intimacy are private and personal matters, so usually, most questions and concerns remain only in our heads.

I write this book to you-for you-to get into your head about it.

I am a reader myself, and I know how it is to be eager to pick up a book about sex and intimacy, then read it and having retained nothing more than what I knew before (because of it being so "text-book safe" and traditional).

I refused to write this book that way. And in order to do so, I had to come out of my shell, reveal some of my secrets and allow you into my head-share the same conversation with you that I have with my close friends about.

So, let's talk about sex. I mean really talk about sex.

The funny thing about us as sexual beings is that as much as we like and love sex, we do not talk about what we really *want* (or want to know about it), we whisper and mostly wonder about it.

This book is dedicated to all adult-minded individuals who want to voyeur inside the bedroom of another's mind while having questions in your own head-wondering if your are pleasing your lover, and taking the time to please yourself and Doing It! (*right*).

Many of the questions, concerns, and desires that we have, tend to be constant conversations that remain only in our heads or perhaps may come up as we share dialogue with our peers-rather than with whom it should concern.

Hopefully, what I discuss in the book will stimulate that conversation in your head and while from afar, and as you read what I say, we are somewhere in this universe telepathically sharing: sharing tangible and practical dialogue while giving you "Mind-Blowing Sex Tips That You Will Never Forget."

I feel confident in saying that by the end of this book, it will add spice to your sex-life: intimately, infinitely.

Enjoy your journey.

With love,

-Angela

# ~HOW to ALLOW this BOOK to STROKE YOU~

This book is about all the informalities; uncovering mysteries behind sexual techniques and how to love yourself and your lover intimately.

Page by page, you will learn what the spiritual and mental connection to the intimate act itself is, when shared with *one* other human being.

There are no mentions whatsoever, about: group-sex, porn or threesomes and such.

The purpose of this book is to teach you techniques about how to have *intimate* se*x* (which is a far cry from the act of merely "having sex,") and definitely the antithesis of aggressive sex and "fucking."

In order to be able to fully understand sensuality and *intimate sex*, you first have to trust the try with yourself (and enjoy it). That is why I begin the book with elaborate tips on how to masturbate yourself and how to masturbate your partner. I then move on to give you tips about how to give your partner the ultimate experience of truly intimate oral-sex (and then from there-I get into actual sexual intercourse tips on how to have  intimate sex between with one another).

As diverse writer who's human in the most natural sense of the word-and sexual being who happens to be an intimacy enthusiast slash closet sensualist; I find that there is a difference between making love, having sex, & "fucking."

None of which, has anything to do with having intimate sex. *Intimate* (masturbation, oral and intercourse) goes a little deeper into the mind. It then connects the body with the self or with one other human being, which is a combination of using your mind with your body, or your mind-*for* their body.

During countless conversations I've had with married persons, though they may be having sex and making love; the intimacy during sex was not there. Many of them had no clue about their partner's bodies in ways outside of a kiss, a touch and entry.

In intimate sex, you are having sex at a pace and with the kind of vulnerability where two people trust one another enough to release their inhibitions and take their time give their lover thorough foreplay and generous deep, motion rather than the swift and selfish (so as to get to know and share their lover's body and intimate sexual response).

Although I am a cheerleader for monogamous relationships and marriage, think of this book like a sandwich with the "meat" in between. Its content is the meat-not the top or bottom piece of bread.

**I do not write about the sexual subjects in this book being specifically being geared for married or monogamous couples (regardless your sexual preference),** because the reality is, people do things mentioned throughout this book without being married or in monogamous relationships. I am not suggesting that if you are not steady with your significant other, these techniques can't be put to use. I am a monogamous-minded spirit-naturally, but despite my delivery; I am not forcing that upon you.

All things considered, do understand that this book is not written to promote promiscuity in any way, shape or form. It is written specifically *to* adults and *for* adults whom I assume have made their own decision about what kind of relation they are involved in.

Bread: You.

Meat: Me.

Book: About sex, sexual techniques & intimacy-period.

Written with the sincerest intention of talking openly about sex, while providing you with unabashed and uninhibited examples of intimate sexual techniques that I guarantee will give you mind-blowing sex tips you will never forget.

No matter what I write about, I only write what I know about, experience, observe or enjoy. I write about what makes me thrive during heartfelt, sincere reciprocated conversation. The subject matters in this book are examples of such things.

All the aforementioned is what I disclaim, now is the time for the "meat" and the pro-claim.

So whether you like it raw, med-well or both; I guarantee you that by the end of this book, you will indeed be: well-done…

# Doing It!

## Mind-Blowing Sex Tips You Will Never Forget

### (The Fine Art of Intimate Sex)

## *TIP 1* ~~~~~~~~~~~~~~~~~~~~~~~~~~~~~~

**MASTURBATION  (Our spiritual "center")**

The subject of masturbation has come a long way, with regard to the "taboo" factor concerning it. Yet, it still has a long way to go. The only "long way" from whence we've come (concerning masturbation) is the fact that we all know, now, that we can't go blind from it. All else, (in the backs of our minds) many of us secretly hold the same taboos since the beginning of time.

People are still embarrassed about it-embarrassed to talk "openly" about it.

It is astonishing-how many men still equate masturbating with a sort of admission that they aren't "getting any."

Equally as astonishing, is how many single women will quickly admit: "I don't masturbate. I have to have the real thing."

When a woman says that, the notion is merely because she hasn't taken the time out to explore pleasuring herself for any length of time, or that she has not uncovered (or been taught) what her options are, with regard to masturbation.

She has everything from devices to stimulate the clitoris to anatomically correct devices that resemble a natural penis.

Men do not have as many options when it comes to sexual self-gratification. A penile suction toy, a makeshift doll with a canal, and a lubricated hand wrapped around his penis is a stark-raving difference from a real vaginal (or anal) canal-neither can be anatomically duplicated, as can a penis.

Before you can understand masturbation and how it [can] work for you, you have to understand that men are women turned inside-out. Meaning: a penis is to a clitoris what his testicle are to our ovaries. Yet, (while giving him head) we can stimulate his testicles (because they are on the outside of his body). Pretty much the only "stimulating" our ovaries get is a monthly period and from conceiving (a child).

But during masturbation, a man doesn't play with his testicles, usually, that does nothing for him-however, he does stroke his penis (clitoris).

During masturbation, with our fingers (or suction/vibrating toys) we play with our clitoris' (those of us who like external stimulation). Others of us may take it a little further and stimulate ourselves internally-with penis-like toys, or actual dildos and such.

## Masturbation is Total Use of the Mental Imagination to Control the Physical Self

Masturbation is mostly mental.

Man or woman, another tool that is essential for masturbation to be of interest to you is your imagination. You have to have a very vivid sexual imagination, and be totally in control of and secure with the fact that no other human being can get into your head and see your actual thoughts but you. All things that you may be too afraid to ask for of your partner, you should at least be able to play them out in your mind, to masturbate-alone. Remember the 3-P's: positions, places and participants, no matter the number, no matter the reality. It's your mind and your moment.

On another note, where masturbation is concerned, like sex and most all things: it begins in the mind.

With that being said, when dealing with *anything* that feeds a hunger (be it sex or food especially), you have to be "on top'" of your mind. When it comes to sex-we are made for it just as much as we are made to eat (to live). It only gets dangerous when we live to eat. So think of your sexual imagination like that. Keep it healthy-no matter how bizarre. As long as your sexual imagination isn't of certain desires that are harmful to other people, go as far as you wish (and take them with you). It doesn't mean that you are a whore if what gets you off quicker is your masturbating to the thought of ten men pleasuring you all at once and from limb-to-limb, anymore than it makes a man a stud-muffin if it gets him off quicker to carrying out the fantasy of pleasuring ten hot women in line-for hours on end.

Use your imagination-just don't let your imagination use you. Do so by considering this rule: if it happens in the mind [it can] happen in time (and that's with anything).

## The "Power" Behind Masturbating

If a woman masturbates, she already knows how to pleasure herself. Masturbation can be a (secret) kind of sexual liberation for a woman in that, if she knows what her body likes and responds to, she will be less inhibited about communicating to her lover what it is she likes-rather than waiting for it to be discovered, at all (if ever)... By the same token, masturbation can be a secret kind of "power," as well.

"Power" meaning, the average (single) woman who masturbates is (usually) less impulsive in her choices and frequency of partners. Masturbation, (especially as we mature), is a kind of spiritual center "controller." When you are in control of your spiritual center (*especially* as a woman), you are more in control of how it is given, what you will accept *at* it, and who you invite to it.

When you masturbate, when courting/dating; you can do so with a clear head, heart and emotions.

Your "spiritual center" won't be pulsating and thinking for you-getting in the way of what's really going on (and what's not). You will understand the difference between loneliness, lust, love or infatuation. Through masturbation, you can save yourself from a whole lot of heartache by paying attention to and knowing how to pleasure your own body. As women, when we are not masturbators, we sometimes find ourselves jumping from partner to partner, impulsion to impulsion, and when that happens, you can't really be so sure that your are being lead by your heart, or the heart in your vagina. Sometimes that "need for companionship" that we *think* we are in need of (even if for an hour) is our vagina talking to us. When that happens, we end up in relationships that our vagina introduced us to, before our hearts our heads stood a chance. And those kinds of relationships grow sour-quickly, or take long roads: hard and harshly.

When you are in touch with your "spiritual center," and are control of it, (when dating) you allow your head to connect with your potential mate's head, your heart to connect to their heart. You are sitting on, tucked away and hidden, what you are in control of.

As a woman, we have a more complex "spiritual center," (our vagina/crouch area).

A man's "spiritual center" is his penis/crouch area.

Generally speaking, during self-pleasure, a man's penis is most important in order for him to reach orgasm during the act, despite the fact how sensitive his testicles, perineum, anus and inner thighs are. (We will cover that in the "Toys for Men" tip coming up).

For a woman, our clitoris is important for reaching an orgasm during masturbation however; some women claim they reach orgasm quicker during vaginal stimulation than they do during clitoral stimulation. Do you want to know what the beauty in that is? There are toys specifically designed for us to get that job done (alone) too. Unlike masturbation devices for men, women have a plethora of self-pleasure options. So, when a: single, grown-up woman says: "I don't masturbate/I need the real thing," it's probably because she either has not taken the time out to explore her own body, or she has not been introduced to the right "toys" and how to use them. And that is where I come in.

**Toys (for women)**

For your information, ladies, there is more out there than "The Rabbit," and that dreaded, played-out, cornball speeding "Bullet" (the one that gets warmer-the longer we leave it turned on). Admit it, we are already afraid to insert that thing; fearing it may break off and get caught inside of our canals. It doesn't do that good of a job for our clitoris' either-mind you. The speed of that little annoying thing nearly feels like the wings of a helicopter fighting your clitoris. It's ridiculous for a little device whose bps (beats per second) that couldn't beat the bps of a cell phones, cause that kind of annoyance huh?

There are two kinds of female masturbators:

-women who are into clitoral stimulation
-women who are into vaginal stimulation

Here are some sure-fire ways that you might enjoy:

Women who are into clitoral stimulation have device options amok in selecting the perfect vibration toys to stimulate her clitoris. The bigger test of whether or not the device is perfect for your own pleasure is simply to buy it, bring it home, and use it.

You can't judge it by how it looks on the box (or what the box says). There are cases where you might buy a device and the bps might not be enough for you-usually those little "cute" and colorful toys are responsible for that kind of let down. With those kinds of devices, you can almost be near a "Scarface" stance; mashing upwards on your poor overworked clitoris while instead of moaning with pleasure: "Say Hello to My Little Friend!"

If you find that you are fighting like that with your new toy-trust me, there are plenty other elves on the shelves that would provide instant pleasure for you-right at the switch of the "on," button.

If you are looking for the very best ones for your  (literal) "bang" with adjustable bps' that are sure to rock your world (and with warm infrared light-I might add); the plug-in-wall kind would be your best bet. Typically, they are massagers (for back and body) but considering that thick, heavy bps and the numerous attachments that come with it, I would image that even during a massage, a woman who wasn't even into masturbation would consider laying a device as such right smack dead in her crouch-you almost can't help but do it.

As far as using the infrared light, I haven't researched what (if any) harm it could do to you while masturbating with the function turned on, but I would recommend using the infrared light only to heat it up so that you can feel enough warmth on your clitoris while you masturbate. The feeling is like a nice warm mouth right on your clitoris.

I know that women that your girlfriends may laugh at you for considering a plug-in-the-wall device, but no matter how "cute" you get with your (other battery-operated) devices-you will find yourself returning back to the plug-in-the-wall ones, I assure you.

**How to Use Masturbating Devices (for her)**

To use these devices, typically, you would lie on your back and open your legs like a frog (or you may leave them closed). You would then place the device on your clitoris, turn the "on" button on and fly to the moon. There's no long drawn-out method. The clitoris is very receptive and submissive. You will figure out how to control it and what works best for you as you feel it.

Some women are into stimulating their clitoris' lying on

their stomachs; rolling over onto their thumbs, using balled-up comforters, blankets, pillows, sides of couches or mattresses. Masturbation is masturbation -what masturbation does: as long as you get to your point of climax-how you get there, is not a major factor.

However, if you want to step it up to the next level of pleasure for you, I would suggest that you try a vibrating device and *then* roll over onto your stomach to masturbate. In doing so, it may lead you to being comfortable enough to lie on your back to masturbate. The difference between lying on your back to masturbate and turning on your stomach to masturbate is mental.
I'll share this much with you.

As a side note (and as a serial life-long masturbator myself) what I noticed (about myself-I do not know how true this may be for you) but, when I was younger- I would roll over and masturbate on my stomach as well. But when I became more comfortable and in tune with pleasuring myself (and different ways to) I was able to do it on my back and legs spread, whether or not it was with my fingers or with a device.

With that being said, if you are still rolling over on your thumb (or any *thing*), try lying on your back and use your fingers to manipulate your clitoris. You can also try lying on your back and masturbate with your balled up sheets or comforters.

No matter *what* you use, the key to this exercise is to try to do it lying on your back.

It brings a different kind of pleasure to you than it does when you roll over on your stomach.

Lying on your stomach to masturbate can be a sign of shame or insecurity.

Masturbation is liberating. So, be and feel liberated while you do it-not shamed or insecure.

It's your alone time, so own that time. Appreciate that time to love and trust yourself. You will, at first, notice that switching from masturbating on your stomach to lying on your back may take quite some time to climax-but allow yourself that time. Turn up the fantasy in your head to the first thing that comes to mind that will send you to instant orgasm (be it oral or intercourse-with whomever or how many comes to mind). It's your mind. It's your body. It's your time. Commandeer that.

For the women who are into vaginal stimulation, you have a different kind of option. Obviously, there are many devices that can be inserted into the vagina to give it pleasure, but for the most-healthiest, I would recommend the good old-fashion dildo. However, unlike being stimulated with the help of another partner caressing and kissing you; masturbating with a dildo (alone) would require that your vagina receive its moisture by way of you. Your sexual imagination is a good tool in securing that. Whatever kind of fantasy you carry on in your head-remember-is yours: the wilder-the better.

To speed up the lubrication process, and of course to get as messy and sloppy as you'd like (seeing as though-you are on your alone time), do *not* feel shame to use a lubricant specifically designed for sexual pleasure. Vaseline, spit and baby oils and such are unspeakably tacky and something I would not recommend at all.

Cherish your pleasure by investing in the proper sexual lubricants to double your pleasure.

If you are not into lubricants of any kind, at the very least, put a lubricated condom on your dildo. That is well over enough lubrication for you along with your mind-to jump start your pleasure-with ease.

### Masturbation Techniques (for her)

Kegel exercising is the act of using only your vagina muscles to contract-contract by: opening/closing, exhaling/inhaling, pushing/pulling.

With Kegel exercises, you do not have to use anything else to do it. Those movements are vagina-exclusive.

If you involve your pelvis or any other movement of your lower half-you defeat the entire purpose of the exercise (which is to tighten the vaginal muscles, however, during the masturbation technique I am about to teach you, using Kegel exercises while masturbating in this way is explosive).

- This 1st technique will involve the use of Kegel exercises *while* the dildo is inside of you:

While on your back, insert the dildo then cross your legs tightly. You can use your fingers to stimulate your clitoris but what works best is vibration-so feel use your massager for your clitoris (for optimum results).

When you do begin to grind your dildo, your vagina muscles should still be constricting that dildo (Kegeling-regardless).

Start off slowly by keeping your grind slow and deep-as if you are trying to keep the dildo inside of you. As the vibration of the massager is stimulating your clitoris while you grind, it will build up sensations in your entire bottom half that you never knew existed when you reach your orgasm (which is at different paces for different women).

The agony of whatever kind of sexual fantasy you are holding in your head combined with the picture in your mind about what's all going on-down below, will steal your intended sexual fantasy away.

It will be a feeling that you will never forget-I assure you.

- This 2nd technique involves nothing but the use of your dildo, you, and the wall:

Many dildos are manufactured in such a way that the bottom end of it will have an opening that, if you squeeze the palm of your hand in it-it will suction your palm (with the air between).

With regard to the gel-like/rubber/plastics materials made for designing the dildo, the force of that suction will allow you to push that dildo against the wall. It will hold itself there as if the wall were a man standing there with a hard-on. Do this with your dildo.

For standing position, after pushing it snug onto the wall, lubricate it with a lubricant specifically designed for sexual activity, or you may put a lubricated condom on it. While standing/knees bent, you can back into it and slowly insert the dildo into your vagina to begin receiving and giving yourself pleasure. It is awesome. Do not be afraid or feel shame. As with your fantasies in your head, you are alone so, commandeer your alone time and own your pleasure.

For squatting position, if you are in your bedroom, you can stick the dildo onto the wall by your bed. Back into the dildo and slowly insert it into your vagina while you are on your knees: doggy-style.

This position gives you better control of the dildo than the standing position does, because your body is more relaxed squatting than it is-standing and kneeling.

Regardless if you are standing or rear-entry, either way, your back is turned to that unforgiving sturdy wall. And once you begin to grind the dildo in and out of you, it will give you the most explosive (and non-stop) pleasure that you will never forget. The good thing about this technique is that, you are in full control of how it will take you to reach orgasm-no rush. No worries.

The pleasure you will feel with this method can nearly drive you up a wall.

Some women are multi-orgasmic and have discovered they are during actual sexual intercourse. With this masturbation technique, and no one to beat you to the orgasm, you are able to see if the same is true for you, so triple your pleasure. Enjoy.

**Masturbating Her**

Masturbating a woman is a little more complex than masturbating a man.

With masturbating a man, the first-basic thought is to grab his penis and start jerking up and down-job done!

In masturbation a woman, the first basic thought (especially for men) is to insert fingers into her vagina and slide in and out-repeatedly.

But when masturbating a woman with your hands, it is best to ask yourself this question: "if another woman would put her hands into the crouch of another woman, what would she do first?' Answer: play with the clitoris, rather than immediately inserting fingers into her vagina.

A woman's vagina is more sensitive in some areas than

others. During the act of having oral-sex performed on her (even from the most inexperienced giver), a wet and busy mouth and tongue will indeed be bound to hit *some* sensitive areas of her vagina that will feel good to her, but the hands are a different kind of pleasure-so you have to know how to be good with them-for her.

Here are some things that you must know:

- When masturbating her with your fingers, you have to make sure you concentrate on her clit and her labia minor (inner lips), because (with fingers) for some women-their clitoris is more sensitive while other women experience more sensation around their inner lips (with fingers). Do not stroke too hard or too fast. Be gentle as if you are trying to make it tickle

- You may play with both her clitoris and her inner lips at the same time with three fingers and three fingers only: your thumb, index and middle finger. Use your thumb to gently circle her clitoris, flip it back and forth as well as rub it up and down, and while doing so, make sure your middle and index fingers are sliding upwards to meet your thumb with every stroke. If you do this repeatedly and well enough, she can get aroused to climax

- Know that while you are in her vagina, women who are right-handed are most sensitive on the right-side of their clitoris and women who are left-handed are more sensitive on the left-side of their clitoris.' Keep that in mind while your thumb is busy

- Though a woman's Mons pubis (the top/fleshy/hairy area of her vagina) as well as her labia major (the thick outer lips) of her vagina are sensitive, when masturbating her-you do not want to make her feel like you are feeling her up as if she is getting a gynecological exam, so at first, stick to her clitoris and inner lips when using your fingers

- When you have aroused her to the point where it should feel good to her to slide your fingers into her vagina, go inside with two fingers and gently wiggle your fingers as if you are asking someone "come here." Most women respond to that technique if you do it in a swift and fast. If done right, it is a jolting good feeling inside of her vagina-especially for women with tilted uteruses-something you can't see [or feel, unless you are a gynecologist]. With that being said, don't go digging trying to "see." Just wiggle your two fingers in that "come here" motion-swiftly and it will drive her crazy.

This technique is one in which you cannot be insecure or scared about doing, so when you go inside-go in like you are going in to find treasure. Wiggle your fingers as if you think you found it, and you're trying to bring it down through her canal. It's an awesome feeling to her.

## Toys (for men)

While women have countless ways to bring themselves sexual pleasure (including the option of having a tool *exactly* like that of a real penis) men do not have a method of self-pleasure that will be exactly like that of an actual canal however, they do have some devices they can use.

## How to Use Masturbating Devices (for him)

There are suction devices that provide warmth while choking and pulsating around the penis.

Many of these devices have holes throughout the inside that secrete warm lubrication onto the penis while in the act of this choking and pulsating sensation given to him to bring him to climax.

Additionally, there are masturbation dolls that are manufactured with canals that can also be lubricated, so that the man can slide his penis into it for self-pleasure. Though a far cry from an actual sphincter or vaginal canal, it will bring him to climax.

## Masturbation Techniques (for him)

The usual and number one option will always be the quickie: lubricating the hand, wrapping it around the penis and jerking it-up and down to bring it to climax. There are some men who do like to be stimulated by anal sex, for masturbation. For him, he too can try the same masturbation technique that I elaborated on under the masturbation for women section: "Masturbation

"Masturbation Techniques"/2$^{nd}$ technique , whereby placing the dildo onto the wall, and putting a lubricated condom on it (or saturating it with a gel or lubricant), he too, can back himself into the dildo while it is being held up by the firm wall. And as well, he too, will experience that same explosive and nonstop pleasure for as long as his heart desires without interruption (or eruption).

## Masturbating Him

Masturbating a man (a hand job/jerking him off) is probably the easiest sexual pleasure of them all-considering the fact that the main focus and object is sitting on the outside of the male body.

While that may be true, a man's penis is more sensitive in some areas than others.

During the act of having oral-sex performed on him (even from the most inexperienced giver), a wet and busy mouth and tongue are bound to hit the right sensitive areas all over a penis during the blow-job. Whereas with a hand job (a good hand job) you have to make sure you do not stroke too hard, or that your stroke isn't too passive either.

A good hand job starts with proper lubrication and knowing whether or not your lover likes it sloppy wet, medium-wet or nearly dry.

The best lubrication is and always will be gels and water-based lubricants that are specifically designed for sexual activity. Spit dries too quickly. Vaseline is too thick a consistency and although it thins out after enough up and down friction, it's still too messy. In giving a man a hand job, using a lubricant that is specifically designed for sexual activity is the best thing you can give him that will be close to the consistency of canal secretion/fluid.

A hand job is not a one-hand job (from start, through to finish). A good hand job requires the use of both hands about as equally as a good *head* job is done with none.

Your hand not only gets tired when you use one hand from start to finish, but (depending on how long it takes for your man to reach orgasm), eventually you will find yourself handling his penis as if it were attached to a non-living and breathing thing, and that is never good.

Instead, try starting off with one hand until you get your rhythm going.

Regardless the curvature of his penis, to give a good hand job (in order for it to be comfortable for him) here are some things that you should know:

- You should omit the word "jerking" out of your mind. It's mental. Substituting the word "jerk" with "stroke" or "stroking" will help you to handle his penis with better care

- You should use your wrist the entire time that you use one hand. This disallows you from mishandling his penis and turning the hand-job

from a stroke to a jerk; pounding his penis up and
down-carelessly

- You should stroke his penis with your thumb loose.
  This ensures you will not find yourself getting
  tired and begin thoughtless jerking, while gripping
  his penis too tight

- The thumb should be constantly stroking the shaft
  (the thick lining or "underbelly" of the penis) as
  your four fingers are stroking it up and down
  (when using one hand)

- You must imagine the letter "c" while stroking it.
  That feels good him and makes it so-you are less
  apt to start *pulling* and jerking his penis versus
  *stroking* his penis (if you are using your wrist, then
  you are doing it right)

- Keep in mind that the shaft of his penis is
  sensitive.
  Every now and again (when you slow stroke) with
  one hand; take your fingernails and gently tickle
  that thick shaft lining beneath it-up and down-
  slowly.
  Using all five of your fingers to trace and gently
  twist at the mushroom head of his penis (as if you
  are screwing a top on the bottle of soda)

- When you stroke his penis using both hands, make sure you use both of your thumbs-stimulating his shaft as stroke, while your four fingers are teasing the opposite/front side of his penis. (To give you a visual, it's as if you are picking up a sandwich with both hands: two thumbs on the bottom of the sandwich, eight fingers on front/top of the bun)

# *TIP 2* ~~~~~~~~~~~~~~~~~~~~~~~~~~~~~~~~~

## WHAT "GOOD SEX" and "GOOD ORAL-SEX" REALLY IS

It's simply: instinctual and mental before it is physical.

Regardless the situation, person or circumstance, the true meaning of "good sex" or "good oral-sex," is merely having the understanding of both acts before any actual person is connected to it (with you).

Understanding "sex" amongst human beings has to be understood in terms of nature and nurture: who we are by nature and what things we do that "nurture" us.

Animals instinctively know what has to be done when the invitation is there.

Human beings have the same instincts, however, our dominion over animals and our ability to be discerning tend to make us ignore who and what we (instinctively) are.

We instinctively make decisions to go at it (intuitively)-first.

That can be a good thing, but when understanding in this order:

-man/woman
-sex (oral or intercourse)

…it can be a "bad" thing, because before understanding sex, we seek to understand the man or the woman first, and then we make them apart of the act of sex.

When to *truly* understand it (sex) and (man/woman) it should be the other way around:

-sex
*…as it relates to*:
-man/woman's (nature)

Understanding man/woman and then sex (with that man or woman) is all well and good in the order of things for romantic love, but even romantic love is "learned" (by way of your reaction to the way it is presented to you). So, with that being said, you have to learn man and woman's sexual *nature* first, and then when you connect with [man or woman] you are able to "nurture" them properly because you have already studied and know how to cater to that man or woman's *true* nature (before they bring to you, all the worldly things that are, and have become).

That is the mental and instinctive way to *behind* knowing what "good sex" or "good-oral-sex" to a man or a woman.

It's not as physical as we think it is. We ignore the instinctual and mental, but when you cater to the mental and instinctual-first, you #WIN.

In short: it's a kind of "pre-meditation." You already know how to please them because you already know how to please their (true) nature. It's like a woman can come to you hard and tough as nails-from the things that she has experienced in the world, yet that is not her *true* nature.

So, when you take her to bed, you do not make love to her "hard and tough as nails self," you take her to bed and make love to her true *nature* and as well, (outside of the bedroom), in spite of her "hard and tough as nails self" you treat her like her true "nature." You can only know how to do those things if you have studied her true nature, before she even came to you…

In our sexual society and culture today, many people are dealing with and "making love" to facades of people; renditions of them rather than catering to that man or that woman's true nature (be it in the bedroom or outside of it).

Men and women are so much alike, yet we are so very different (in terms of nature-nurture).

With regard to sex, a man's nature is responsive to servitude and "giving"

Their sexual nature is to be "taken in."

Women are responsive to gratitude and to be "given to"

Their sexual nature is to be "taken."

So when in an act of something as instinctive as sex, that has to be your approach-with that man or that woman (regardless their persona when they come to you).

No matter *how* "broke" a man may be mentally, emotionally or financially, his nature responds to being catered to a certain kind of way (in or outside of the bedroom). And if you cannot meet that, then you really have not met *him*-you are dealing with some caricature him.

With regard to sex, as mentioned earlier, good sex it is not just a physical experience.

It is mental and instinctual, first. You have to "think" your sex through without delivering it mechanically.

After you have done the "thinking" as elaborated at the beginning of this chapter tip, you then attach the person's nature and then their person to the sex.

That is when the physical comes in.

When you tailor your sexual style to that person's [male or female nature first] then with their sexual style and what nurtures them-then good sex and good oral-sex happens.

I won't belabor the obvious any longer.

"Technique" *does* indeed play a part in "good-sex" and "good oral-sex" as well (which I thoroughly teach and elaborate on in chapter Tips 3, 4 and 5), but just like the point of *this* chapter tip: you have to start from *the bottom*; the rooter to the tooter, to get to the nature of a thing before it blossoms.

Then you'll get the ripe (and right) fruit of that thing.

With that being said, turn the page, let's eat:

## TIP 3 ~~~~~~~~~~~~~~~~~~~~~~~~~~~~~~~~

**ORAL-SEX**
**(For her)**

Oral-sex for her-definitely starts in her mind.

Regardless her persona outside of the bedroom, whether she is feminine, tomboy or a stud; when in preparation for oral-sex, be gentle with her, because for any woman who's made comfortable enough to feel like her vagina is a special delicacy and beautiful work of art; oral-sex is explosive.

A woman may allow you to taste her vagina, but a woman will *relax* and allow you into her vagina for as long as you like and however you like *after* you have done the head work with her first. Not so much as "head work" as in conversation (only); but head work in that, in every subtle or overt way, she needs to know that you absolutely love her vagina.

Whether it's the way you grope or touch her vagina or the way you caress her vagina with your hands, and if you literally communicate to her-that you love her vagina; she will relax and be more receptive to you in more ways than many.

Once you have that out the way, even if your performance was less than stellar-she will let you try again, but if you did not let her know that you loved and appreciated her vagina, but you still somehow made your way down there-and you weren't that good, don't count on her allowing you back in.

Because as a woman, though she may not tell you, in the back of her mind, she will wonder if your terrible performance had anything to do with the anatomy of her vagina or if it had anything to do with her scent or taste, and for her, the best way to deal with it is to not allow you back to that very private and personal part of her again-unless you can do a good job of convincing her otherwise (the head work).

As mentioned in the "Masturbating her" tip, a woman's vagina is her spiritual center. Having a face in her vagina is a top-of-the-line spiritual experience because of the vulnerability involved.

If she knows that you enjoy the look, smell, touch and taste of her vagina combined with the fact that you touch her in all the right places-she is yours forever; both-spontaneously and intimacy unplanned.

Let her know that you need it before you eat it and she'll trust you on a different level with her (intimately).

**The Anatomy of it All**

For oral-sex pleasure, a woman's vagina contains six important parts:

- Her Mons Pubis (the top/fleshy/hairy area of her vagina)
- Her Clitoris (located atop the vagina just beneath the outer lips and connected to the inner lips)
- Her Labia Major (the thick outer lips of the vagina)
- Her Labia Minor (the thin inner lips/folds of the vagina that extend from the clitoris & has right and left flaps/wings)
- Her Hymen (located underneath the inner lips-surrounding the opening/hole of her vagina)
- Her Vaginal Opening

Additionally, these things are a must (from you). Your:

- Lips
- Tongue
- Teeth

**How to Pleasure the Vagina and Where to Play**

A woman's vagina is a complex work of art, and is responsive in different ways, while different things are being done to it. As I mentioned in the "Masturbating her" chapter tip, your fingers stimulating her vagina is one thing, but your mouth on her vagina is an altogether different kind of experience.

With your mouth on her vagina, she and her vagina are at your mercy.

In addition to her being in a vulnerable state of emotion; a vagina is so sensitive that, to have a warm mouth, lips and tongue manipulating it is one of the best sexual experiences a woman can receive.

Although different women's vaginas are more responsive in certain areas than others, one thing they all have in common is that once you have manipulated *all* areas from the "Anatomy of it All" (above listed), her whole vagina will be responsive, sensitive and aroused.

**Oral-sex Tips (for performing oral-sex on her)**

These are some tips on how you pleasure a woman's vagina. Pay attention:

> 1. Do not spend the entire time playing with her clitoris with the tip of your tongue without involving your lips to suck and pull at it while pleasuring her. While the constant flickering of a speeding tongue can be arousing, too much of it- the entire way through-can be annoying. Do not misconstrue her screams and moans with the fact that she likes it.

While she may have liked it from the start, it becomes uncomfortable if you give her the "hurricane tongue" for too long a time. At some point in the middle of that kind of stimulation on a clitoris, she needs you to "take her"-so, it is absolutely imperative that you devour her clitoris in between those speedy strokes of your hurricane tongue-to tease and balance the pleasure. Stop and take her clitoris into your mouth with your lips and give her nice deep and slow pulls.

You will hear her gasp with the kind of pleasure that will let you know that you are doing her right. After giving her your hurricane tongue for a while, it is a relief to her-to be taken (by devouring her clitoris). If a woman grabs hold of your head and thrusts her pelvis upwards when you take her clitoris into your mouth-pay attention, because that means she wants you to keep your entire: mouth, tongue and lips on her clitoris.

2. When you are performing oral-sex on a woman, get your hands involved at times within the act. While it may be true that the best oral-sex performed on a man is without hands, the same does not hold true for performing oral-sex on a woman. Open her outer lips with your fingers, and take her clitoris into your warm mouth-give it your "divided" attention-like you mean business about it.

When you use more than just the tip of your tongue to pleasure a woman's clitoris-you are letting her know that you *enjoy* eating her. Sending a speeding tongue around her vagina; flipping about over her clitoris the entire time you are performing oral-sex on a woman conveys a sexual message that you are either: scared, new at this, do not enjoy her vagina, or all three.

4. With the tip of your tongue, treat the entire length of her clitoris and both sides of her inner lips like a package deal, but place most of the emphasis on her clitoris.

When stimulating a woman's clitoris, keep in mind (as stated in the "Masturbating her" tip), a woman's right side of her clitoris is more sensitive to her if she is right-handed and more sensitive on the left side if she is left-handed. So when you have your mouth over her clitoris, while you are sucking it; turn your head sideways and slide your mouth up and down her clitoris' right (or left side) in between the times you are manipulating her clitoris with your tongue. Be sure to manipulate your tongue deep and up and down that right (or left side) of her clitoris. Take time to hold her open and trace the lining of both sides of her inner-lips with the tip of your tongue (tickle it).

This makes her clitoris even more aroused.

Always remember this one thing about a vagina: any place you play in it (with your tongue) sends blood-flow and sensation to her clitoris. So whenever you play anywhere else, a woman loves when we re-visit her clitoris. It's like a build-up of pleasure. To make her climax (hard), isolate her clitoris by keeping it locked in your mouth while giving her swift tongue strokes. Use your entire head and face to "fuck" her (with deep slow thrusts). That will drive her crazy.

5. Keep in mind that it is never a good idea (nor is it arousing) to just open a woman's legs and start right in on sucking her love juices at her vaginal opening.

If you turn back to the "Anatomy of it All" list, take notice of how the "vaginal opening" is listed last, that is because if you take the time to pleasure a woman's entire vagina and you want her vaginal opening to be aroused and sensitive to your mouth, it would be best to pleasure her in that list's order: from top (Mons pubis) to bottom (vaginal opening). You must stimulate the vaginal areas above the vaginal opening in order for her vaginal opening to be aroused.

6. Keep in mind that the proper way to pleasure her vaginal opening is not a raunchy act of trying to suck all the juices out of it. That's a turn-off to a

woman. Screams from her (when that happens) are most likely screams of shock and awe. The proper way to pleasure her vaginal opening is to treat it like that French kiss that you would give her mouth (on her face). Except while you are at her vaginal opening, treat the opening like that dreaded (mouth-to-mouth) deep-throated tongue action that makes *any*body a "bad-kisser" for doing so. With your face in her vagina, that kind of "bad kiss" *is* acceptable, mouth-to-mouth: never. Additionally, that swift and constant hurricane-tongue action is fair game at her vaginal opening. The best way to give you a visual as to how you should pleasure her vaginal opening is for you to imagine your tongue as having more than one function. A strong, swift tongue that is behaving like a penis along with your mouth; softly French-kissing her vaginal opening is awesome. That is the proper way to bring pleasure to it.

7. Do not ignore that fatty/spacious area atop her vagina (the Mons pubis). You can play with that area while beginning to pleasure her, by gently sucking and biting on it like you would her clitoris-and give it some teeth. Not hard, but lovingly. Make her feel like her vagina is a delicacy to you. As you make your way from the Mons pubis down to the vaginal opening, occasionally make your way back up to the Mons

pubis. Gentle bites, suction and kisses feel awesome there, once the whole vagina has been stimulated. Tease her, switch up.

8. If you are pleasuring a woman in every way that I explained in those seven tips-you are definitely: #WINNING!

9. This next step is for the adventure-seeker. If you are feeling mighty and want to take it a step higher, do know that her anal opening can be treated just like I explained her vaginal opening should be stimulated (in #6). So that you may keep this technique apart from her vagina, you may want to go to her anal opening right after she has climaxed from your pleasuring her vagina. While she plateaus, you can pleasure her there (rim/toss her salad) if she is not opposed to it. It is not a useless sexual act. It feels about as awesome to a woman to be rimmed as it does for a man.

## The Mental Versus Physical Aspect of Performing Oral-Sex on Any Woman

To further extend your gratitude to her for allowing you to have that special part of her, there are several other oral-sex positions in which you can have her. They not only turn her on and make her weak while in the sexual act; but they heighten this moment of oral-sex intimacy for her-by being "taken" in these ways that I am about to show you.

No matter what type of woman she is: feminine, tomboy, or even a stud; a woman is at her sexual weakest when she allows someone to perform oral-sex on her.

That being said, she is at your mercy and is an emotional rag-doll while allowing you into her spiritual "center." If you are to pleasure her thoroughly, you must "capitalize" on that moment from time to time-do more than just lie in front of her and eat her senseless.

I am going to list some ways to take her higher, but don't be a glutton and an acrobat either by trying to do them all in one night. That can be more annoying than it is pleasurable for a woman.

Do not interrupt the moment of passion she is experiencing all to show her how creative you can be all in a night. Instead, take your pick.

Work it (and her) and then save some for later.


**Oral-sex Positions (for performing oral-sex on her)**

Here are some mentally intense ways to take her higher. It is a combination of mind-fucking her, while "fucking" her (with your mouth):

## *Panties Pulled to the Side*

To pull a woman's panties to the side in preparation for oral-sex, heightens the experience in that it gives off a sense that there is a rush to get to her-yet, you cannot wait to pull her panties down and take them off, so instead-you pull them to the side to start in her. The actual act is no different than you would if her panties were off of her body. Allow her to experience the feeling of you not being able to wait to get to her-by taking your hand and hold her panties off to the side. It will drive her crazy.

Do not make her do anything besides open up her legs to you, to allow you to enjoy what you are doing to her (all for her pleasure). It's mental. This experience will force her to surrender to you in ways that she won't quite understand. Subconsciously, it feels like a sexual quickie and rush-job coming on, but the way you are making her feel should be no such way-do it right, nice, deep and slow-like you mean business about her vagina. With her panties pulled to the side, she is concentrating on climaxing as fast as she can but you should merely be concentrating on making her cum as hard as she can. When her subconscious thoughts meet what you are conscious of-it is explosive.

## *Edge of the Table (while you sit)*

To place a woman at the edge of the table to eat her is perfect. In her subconscious mind, she'll be even more excited because she will know that you *really* like eating her pussy-so much so that you are willing to sit her on the edge of a table as if she were a delicacy. Always keep in mind about what I mentioned at the start of this "Oral-Sex: for her," chapter: after she is convinced that you love her pussy (the smell, the taste and the anatomy of it), her confidence expands and therefore, her legs will open even wider for you, and with your face in her vagina-you can take her anywhere you want to.

Place her on the table-comfortable for her, but close enough to the edge so that you can eat her like a good meal. In this oral-sex position, she will know that you feel honored to be pleasuring her. Although it *looks* like you are in the submissive position from which you are eating; she is *actually* the one submitting unbeknownst to her. Though the table is not a very comfortable position for her (for a long period of time), before you know it, she will be arched and laid back-in screams of passion-trying hard to meet your mouth with the best orgasm she can thruster (while trying to fight that uncomfortable position across that table, about as equally as she is loving what you are doing to her). Bon' appetite!

### *While She Stands and Straddles You*

This oral-sex position is best performed with your back up against the wall and the lady facing the wall. Typically, oral-sex in this stance happens in a spontaneously "natural" moment. Perfect for that moment when she not very happy with you for whatever reason and you hold her, kiss and caress her all the way down her body, and fall to your knees in a corner for comfort. Then you hold her waist and kneel between her legs-stretching yours enough to open her legs around yours. By the time you are into pleasuring her, her forehead should have hit the wall and your face should be right into her crouch: snatching, pulling and eating at her until you have her to the point where she is practically grinding the back of your head into the wall. You should be able to gauge her arousal by her grind, and the way she is trying to hold her standing position.

What's good about this technique is not so much that it is uncomfortable, but also because it is a woman's nature to want to be held or cuddled and to feel "secure." Standing with her face to the wall and being pleasured in such a way beneath her, gives her no security for the entire back of her body, and nothing but a corner of a wall in front-to support her. The only "security" she will feel is your grasp (whether it be on her hips, her buttocks or her thighs). It's mental. The agony of nothing covering and securing her from behind will force her to thrust and grind towards your face in such a way, that she will help bring that orgasm *to* you.

(If you are pleasuring her in any way like I explained in #'s 1-7 "How to Pleasure the Vagina and Where to Play") don't be surprised if she has a lock on your head with her hands.

### *While She Sits and Straddles You*

In oral-sex, to place a woman above you is a mind-blowing experience for her, (especially if you catch her by surprise when you do it).

A "catching her by surprise" example could mean that the two of you are lying there having regular conversation while she just happens to be straddled over you-looking down at you. Or it could very well be in the middle of her sexing you while she's on top. Without her expecting it, simply grab her ass almost like you are smacking it. Hold her firmly (as if she had better not refuse what you are about to do), and treat her like she is a piece of delicacy that you have been waiting to eat all day. It will drive her crazy.

This technique is a little startling, however in the middle of that sexual or intimate moment that she is straddled on top of you, when she is interrupted from the pleasure of that intimate moment (of conversation or intercourse), and suddenly grasped in such a dominant way; she will be caught in between thoughts of not wanting to ruin the moment by declining to sit on your face, as well as being intimidated by the position-altogether. That weakens her. It's mental. Once you get her comfortably on top of your face (whether she squats, sits/ride you, or rolls on all fours to cover your face with you in-between her legs), she will work hard to meet you half-way on getting that orgasm to her. She can't help but to.

-

### *From the Rear (while she is on all fours)*

The good thing about this position is that it can *begin* with her standing and straddling your face (as explained in: "While She Stands and Straddles You").

It could then lead right into her sitting and straddling your face (as explained right before this section in: "While She Sits and Straddles You"). You could then finish her off from the rear while she is on all fours with you pleasuring her from behind.

This position is most comfortable for her when her chest area is placed flat to the bed (or floor). Doing so makes her toot her bottom more erect, which gives you greater access to her vagina. With you in between her legs from the rear-she will of course have to squat and open her legs some-to allow you to reach her clitoris.

Keep this in mind: all women's vagina's are not all built the same. They have shorter or longer crouch lengths (the length from the Mons-pubis back to the anal opening). Some women can squat and toot her bottom right out and her entire pussy is right there in your face from behind: clit as visible as her vaginal opening. Other women, you have to go further under her to reach her clitoris-(which means she'll be squatting with her legs slightly wider in order to let you in between to get at it).

So that you don't embarrass yourself and make this about

as messy an experience as you can make it embarrassing for her, when you get her on all fours, just gently (and with a little bit of sexiness, I might add) push her back all the way down until her chest hits the bed or floor. Make sure she is tooted out. When she is, take your hand and cuff her entire vagina-play with it for a little bit for her… but really…you should be gauging how far she is going have to spread in order for you to get your mouth on that clitoris.

This is also a good position that, if you have pleasured her good enough from the Mons-pubis down to her vaginal opening (as explained in: #5, 6 & 7 under: "How to Pleasure the Vagina and Where to Play") no matter how lengthy her crouch is-to give you access to her clitoris from this position-her vaginal opening will be right there in your face. So, if you wish to French kiss her vaginal opening in a way that will blow her mind, doing it from the rear gives you better access to deep tonguing and French-kissing it than it does with you facing it.

If you have aroused her (as explained in: #5, 6 & 7), she will nearly lose control of herself while you pleasure this way. While pleasuring her vaginal opening from behind, masturbate her clitoris with your hand, or better yet, make *her* masturbate her own clitoris while you tongue and French-kiss her vaginal opening. With her lying comfortably on her chest, she will be able to do it with both of her hands. Hopefully, she's already a masturbator, because this will drive her insane as she reaches climax. If she is not, make her masturbate herself anyway, because you already have work to do from behind.

You will love it and she will never forget it.

For my adventure-seekers, if while back there French-kissing & tonguing her love juices, you are feeling even more adventurous; feel free to pleasure her anal opening by French-kissing and tonguing it (the way that I explained in the "How to Pleasure the Vagina and Where to Play" section #9). As she is masturbating her own clitoris for you; having you behind her giving her twice that kind of pleasure will indeed drive her insane.

## TIP 4 ~~~~~~~~~~~~~~~~~~~~~~~~~~~~~~~~~~~

**ORAL-SEX**
**(For him)**

Oral-sex for him-starts the very moment you kneel to pleasure him.

Regardless his persona outside of the bedroom, whether he is effeminate, the average male or a manly-man; unlike oral-sex for a woman; men do not harbor the same *kinds* of thoughts (where oral-sex is concerned). Men really *need* oral-sex.

Men and women are reached intimately in different ways-different ways meaning, whereas oral-sex is not so "essential" to reach a woman intimately, it *is* essential in reaching a man intimately. (I did not say that oral-sex is essential to reaching a man "emotionally." I said that oral-sex is essential in reaching a man "intimately." There is a difference). It's not so much about the necessity being some burning desire or emotional pre-requisite, and although they may not express it to you, men *need* oral-sex to the extreme that if you are going to be sexually intimate with a man and you are not going to perform oral-sex on him, you almost shouldn't be sexually intimate with him at all.

For men (unlike for women) pleasuring his penis is pleasuring a part of "him;" his "person," his: male-hood.

Men are fighting a different kind of fight in this world (with regard to gender roles and expectations).

No matter how educated, spiritually grounded or resilient they are in their fight not to be defined by certain expectations of them as a male in order to claim his role as a "man;" all men know that their money (or lack thereof) along with subcategories such as: car, job, other materialisms and societal expectations do define him (in the world's eyes).

All men are aware of the *expectation*-even if they reject it. They all know that having money is looked upon being powerful and masculine: something that suits and is expected of their role as a "man" in this world.

Opposite but equal as that, a man also knows that his penis holds a kind of "power." I would jokingly add that if it didn't, how or why is it massively manufactured and duplicated the world over, impressively more anatomically correct and precise than any "anatomically correct" vagina has ever been manufactured?

But unlike money and the subcategories beneath it, a penis has no subcategories beneath it-it is what it is. The only expectation beneath it is: you…

Not only is it his "spiritual center" (as a woman's vagina is-hers), a lot of physiological, social, psychological, mental and emotional strings are attached to a man's penis. One of the best forms of appreciation, admiration and respect that you can bestow upon a man is through his penis (oral-sex).

Even if for an hour, through oral-sex, a male could be made to feel like a "man" when the world tells him otherwise (for any lack there-of's), and as well (or otherwise) a "better" man.

**The Anatomy of it All**

For oral-sex pleasure, a man's penis contains six important parts:

- His Glans Head (the mushroom head with the thick lining atop the penis and an opening at the center)
- His Frenulum (the area underneath the back of the head where the shaft begins)
- His Shaft (the thick almost "muscular" looking lining underneath the penis that extends beginning underneath the back of the penis just beneath the Glans head)
- His Foreskin (the skin all around the penis near the Glans head. "Meaty" and fleshier when it is flaccid/not hard (on a circumsized man). And when uncircumsized, this area covers the entire

Glans head

- His Testicles (attached to the bottom of the penis). This sack contains two scrotums. Some men have one, due to surgery or other conditions, however, whether they have one or two; the sensation during pleasuring a man's testicles is the same for either man)
- His Perineum (not exactly considered a part of the penis-but rather, a part of the sensation in the prostate sensation. Located just beneath the testicles, if you lift them, the perineum is that area of fleshy thick space of "nothing" before the anal cavity begins)

Additionally, these things are a must (from you). Your:

- Lips
- Tongue
- Teeth

## How to Pleasure the Penis and Where to Play

A man's penis is not complex because of its anatomy. Its complex work of art is in knowing where to bring pleasure to its simple areas by knowing: how much pressure to apply to it, the rhythm you must develop, and consistency in that rhythm.

As I mentioned in the "Masturbating him" chapter tip, stroking his penis is one thing, but your mouth on his penis is an altogether different kind of experience.

Unlike with oral-sex with a woman (where, with your mouth on her vagina she is at your mercy); with your mouth on a man's penis you are at his mercy.

Oral-sex for a man doesn't necessarily put him in a "vulnerable" state of emotion, but rather, makes him feel appreciated, validated, accepted and "taken-in" by you.

It's mental. Not (just yet) emotional.

It is a relief of a release for him-almost like any pressures or stresses of the day or the world are coming through him, by way of his penis-to you: beneath him, at: it.

To have a warm mouth, lips and tongue manipulating it, is one of the most explosive experiences a man can have. He anticipates that explosive moment and what is going to be done with it-at that ("explosive") moment. In the back of his mind, he wonders how you are going to receive him in the end. The turn-on for him is the anticipation and from not having to ask you what you are going to do with it. Usually, he hopes and waits to find out about as much as he hopes for an awesome blow-job being given to him-leading up to it.

The beauty of perfect oral-sex with a man versus perfect oral-sex with a woman is that, if you manipulate a woman's vagina from the literal top (Mons pubis) to the very bottom (vaginal opening), you get better results, in that her vagina responds like light bulbs being turned on as you lick, suck and manipulate each part from the top to the bottom.

By the time you get to the bottom (vaginal opening), she is lit. From there you can manipulate her vagina anywhere from there, and then start your own rhythm, because she will be responsive to every lick, suck and touch.

It's slightly different with a man.

I cannot teach you "rhythm" with a man unlike with a woman. You are in control of your rhythm with a woman because her vagina is passive, and lays there for you to take control of it.

A man's penis is considered "aggressive" because it is atop his body and can move about.

Although you have to control it too, you do so by establishing your own rhythm, which is all a matter of his penis length and girth, the structure of his penis (curved up, down, left , right, straight) as well as how far you are willing to go while in the act.

Your own rhythm is found through handling all of that while in the act.

In thinking about the light-bulb example I just mentioned about how a woman's vagina is fully aroused by manipulating it from top to bottom; with a man (thanks to nature), he is already about a third of the way aroused once his penis is on-hard.

He has one whole light-bulb; lit and ready for you-so you can start from top to bottom, sideways, locked inside of the side of your jowl, at his testicles, on his penises head, the shaft, swift strokes all around his penis-or wherever you wish to.

## Oral-sex Tips (for performing oral-sex on him)

Although a man's penis is aroused easily, hard and ready to assist you; you still have some work to do to arouse *him*. These are some tips on how to pleasure a man's penis. Pay attention:

> 1. To get a good rhythm going, in your mind, you need to be familiarizing, exploring and acquainting yourself with how he is built.

> Your tongue and lips should be doing a kind of dance around the mushroom (head) of his penis and taking swift, sharp, deep strokes around the entire rim of the head of his penis while you hold it in your mouth.

> 2. When giving head, don't be so stiff that you refuse to move your own head; it makes it easier for you, and makes it more pleasurable to him. Be natural with it and take your time at first. Don't be instant bobble-head. That kind of arousal (in you) should take a little time (if you are properly exploring his penis with your mouth, tongue and lips and getting aroused in the process).

Concentrate on his penis being the object of your mouth, lips and tongue's business. Be serious about what you are doing. This is an important "job" for him-and as well, it should be for you. Once you get your rhythm going, your head and neck will relax and swing around his pole with pleasure.

3. If you give a blow-job with too stiff a head and neck-you are more apt to pull at it and more inclined to get your teeth involved. If you loosen up some, you too, will enjoy using your tongue, lips and mouth, and within that first sixty-seconds that you didn't scare him or make him jump; he will relax and begin to trust that you are about to give him complete thorough pleasure.

4. Why the "first sixty-seconds?" A man can tell if you give good head within about the first sixty-seconds of doing it, and in that time; he can tell if you are really enjoying what you are doing. Sixty-seconds is about the amount of time you get to establish a rhythm and give him permission to relax, while having your mouth on his penis. More than they will ever admit to, men are most anxious at the beginning of getting a blow-job (no matter how many times he's had one). He will be anxious the whole way through if your performance was less than stellar-despite the fact that he will ejaculate; he will ejaculate regardless-that still

does not mean it was a job well-done. When you concentrate on merely making him cum, you cannot give a good blow-job. He does not need your help in concentrating on his ejaculation; your focus should be on all the things leading to giving him a good orgasm-like a volcano erupting. You: be and do the things that cause the volcano to erupt.

5. If you keep your hands out of the way, you are more apt to use your tongue, lips, mouth and head a lot better, and offer better play. A good blow-job must be done with all tongue, lips and no teeth-best: with no hands. Under no uncertain terms should a man feel the ridges of your teeth on his penis, no matter how gentle you think you can be in doing so. Men are very sensitive about their penises in every way. They literally guard it with their life-even with their clothes on. So in giving a good blow-job, he is unclothed (go figure). There is absolutely no room in a man's mind to entertain the thought of having to guard his penis while you have your mouth on it. That is much too disturbing for his mental in this moment. He just wants you to give him pleasure, not make him think, instruct, or have you proceed by his caution. The only time your teeth may be felt during a blow-job is when you are giving a man head with a condom on-and yet and still, there is a certain way that you have to do that (which I will elaborate on at the end of the

book under the "Using Sexual Protection" chapter Tip 8).

6. The shaft of a man's penis is one of the essential parts of giving an awesome blow-job.

If, while you are in the middle of your rhythm, you find yourself sucking up and down on him; that motion should never be done without your tongue providing him with swift spiraling strokes up and down his shaft-from every which direction possible, while he fits firmly between your mouths lips. In between this motion, tease him by discontinuing your tongue action; folding your teeth behind the gum of your mouth and using your folded lips to go up and down on his penis. Rotate between this and using your tongue to spiral him, while his penis is inside of your mouth.

Keep in mind that with your mouth/lips folded over his penis, riding up and down it; you will have a nice grip on it. You may feel a compulsion to grip his penis extremely tight. There *is* such a thing as sucking him too tight. That is not comfortable for him. Do not think of sucking him with the pressure of "flattening" his penis. Think of sucking him with enough pressure that it is tight enough in your mouth where you can still feel the natural width of his girth as you grasp, lick, spiral, and fold while going up and down on him.

When you are ready to slide off his penis, be prepared to try a different angle with his penis still trapped in your mouth like the next technique.

7. This next technique is for non-braces wearers. When you have a good rhythm going (as explained in #6), you can still give his penis the same pleasure of being trapped inside of your mouth. However, with the method, you will slide his penis to the side-in between your jowl and side teeth. If you are right-handed, it is probably more comfortable to slide it on the right-side of your jowl, left-side of your jowl if you are left-handed. That is because if you are right-handed; with his penis trapped between your right jowl and side teeth, with your tongue; you will be able to give him swift, deep strokes on his penis while you use your (literal) head and face move about horizontally. This make makes his penis ride the ridges of your side-teeth while your tongue is doing its own dance. He will enjoy it, immensely.

8. For those moments during your blow-job when when you raise off his penis and you're licking, kissing and sucking, rather than entrapping it in your mouth; keep in mind, this tip about a *circumcised* man's Frenulum: the area located atop and behind the penis head-at the beginning of the shaft is either one of two things for a man: with the sensitivity equal to a woman's clitoris or too

sensitive to touch. Some men's foreskin is tighter in that area than other men. The best way to test his response to this area, while you are pleasuring his penises head in your mouth, is to take a few swift strokes around the thick mushroom head. Wrap your tongue underneath the start/back of the head of his penis and tease it briskly (while your mouth is pleasuring his penises head). If you can tell that is not irritating him, you should proceed to tease and French kiss his Frenulum while teasing his penises head.

For the *uncircumcised* man, that technique is one of the best things you can do for him, because the majority of the time, a man's penis is in a flaccid state. Even in that flaccid state (on the circumcised male), his penises head is visible, whereas on the uncircumcised man; his penises head is completely covered and buried in the extra uncut foreskin. Because of that, the uncircumcised man's penis head and Frenulum is near virginal and is definitely responsive to stimulation-so you can love all on it for a long period of time. However, do not forget the rest of his penis (circumcised or uncircumcised).

Occasionally slide your tongue up and down the shaft of it and use your mouth to French-kiss the shaft, too-in between your tongue-play.

9. While you are giving him head, do not forget that his testicles are highly sensitive. By this time in the blow-job, they should be good and warm and relaxed; which means the skin on his sack should be loose-therefore you can get full access to his balls for your mouth. The trick to this technique is to take each testicle and play with each one as if you have blown a bubble with bubblegum, and trying not to bust the bubble. The sound should be like a whipping or slurping sound. Your tongue should be moving swiftly back and forth as if you are trying to balance his ball while in your mouth. Give each ball some play, and on occasion, take them both in your mouth and divide them with your tongue. Do this technique a few times-he will love it.

10. When you are ready to, come off of his balls and use your tongue to firmly press his sack's skin back into his perineum-which too, is very sensitive. Here, you can apply as much pressure as you like-because it tickles his prostate.

11. When you are ready to pleasure his perineum from behind his testicle sack, carefully lift the sack (with your face/nose) and go underneath. You will probably have to open his legs slightly wider-with his knees up some, in order for you to get full-access to his perineum.

When your tongue reaches it, you will know you are in the right place. It's merely fleshy and thick-right underneath his testicles. While there, you can have a lot of fun. He will enjoy it-immensely. Spend time French-kissing his perineum, pressing and wiggling your tongue as if you are trying to break through the skin. You can do this as firmly as you'd like, because no matter how hard your wiggle and press; it will not break the skin. This pressure however, tickles his prostate in ways that even he won't understand. He'll just know that it feels awesome, so have fun applying pressure down there with your mouth, tongue and lips. Additionally, it feels awesome to take your fingers to press and massage his perineum. Men can reach climax from this having being done to them, alone.

12. For my adventure-seekers, the ultimate (sexual) prostate-tickling experience for a man is his anus. His "G-spot" is located there. Deep tonguing and French-kissing his anus gives him one of the most explosive sexual experiences a man can have. If you are, what I will refer to as "adventure-seeker-lite," rather than to stick your tongue there, (if your lover allows you) you can stick your fingers there-instead. One, but no more than two fingers will do. The proper way to pleasure his anus with your fingers is by gently inserting (it-the index finger) or them (the index

finger and middle-finger) inside. Once inside, at
the finger tip/first finger line, as you slide further,
begin to wiggle your fingers at a medium speed
and as if you are signaling "come here." When you
are all the way in (even if only in to the second
lines of your fingers) you can continue this motion
throughout, and he will enjoy it immensely. Don't
just lay there and listen and stare, give him some
great head while you finger him. At best, use your
thumb to massage his perineum in the middle of all
this-he will be near delirious. When you find that
he is enjoying the pleasure you are giving him, you
can speed up your finger wiggling motion-and
don't be surprised if he cums: hard, because he
will, indeed.

13. Speaking of cumming hard. When a man is
about to climax, his penis pulsates as if a heart is
beating right inside of it. Now is the time for you
to decide what you are going to do about it. At
best, for him, the ultimate feeling is to have your
entire mouth devouring it while he climaxes. While
devouring, the act of gripping it and providing
lightning speed spiraled strokes across the back of
the shaft while sucking up and down on it as he is
ejaculates (inside of your mouth)-drives him up a
wall. Whether you swallow or hold it in your
mouth to spit out after he's done is not as
important to him as you taking him in (your
mouth). The point of ultimate satisfaction for him

is that he ejaculates in a mouth that is devouring his penis-point blank. If you cannot swallow but want to give him that pleasure, hold it on your mouth until he's done ejaculating, and spit it out when he's done.

14. If you cannot stomach the feeling of having him ejaculate in your mouth, but you want him to still get the feeling of you having done so you will need your hands at this point. While you are devouring his penis and gripping it and providing it with lightning speed spiraled strokes across the back of the shaft while sucking up and down on it, when he begins to pulsate, you must be prepared to rise up off of it. There are two ways to do it: with one hand or with both of your hands.

With one hand: in a position with the back of your hand facing you-take your thumb and index finger and grip it just underneath his mushroom-like a ring. Use the inside of your hand as a kind of "shield" to cuff his entire penis head inside the palm of your hand. Use your palm and remaining three fingers to cover and massage his penises head while he is ejaculating inside your palm.

With both hands: encompass his penises head in between both of your hands, with both of your thumbs visible. Move your thumb gently about-occasionally kneading his Frenulum with it.

The object of this technique is to contain his ejaculation and enclose the head. You have to figure out which way is most comfortable for you-naturally.

The key to pleasuring him with this one and two hand technique is to give him the feeling that he ejaculated inside of something. Rather than having ejaculated inside of your warm mouth, it is inside of your warm hands-safe from your mouth and traveling down his penis, because as your hands do the devouring of his penis head, make sure you use your mouth, lips and tongue to whip aggressively up and down his penises shaft and around his entire penis itself-so as to make it feel warm and wet as he is ejaculating (in your hands). He will love it.

15. If the above two (#'s 13 & 14) are not for you, then you definitely should be giving him head with a condom on-the whole way through. I will explain how to do that at the end of the book under the "Using Sexual Protection" chapter Tip 8. The reason why I say you should be giving head with a condom on the whole way through is because as I explained earlier: a man anticipates his explosive moment and what is going to be done with it-at that moment. That "explosive" moment is his point of ejaculation. In the back of his mind he wonders how you are going to receive him in the end.

The turn-on, his anticipation-is from not having to ask you. Usually, he hopes and waits to find out about as much as he hopes for that awesome job being done on him-leading up to it. That "awesome" job-leading up to it is one thing, but that awesome job is an awesome job well-done, if you receive him in the end (whether it is in your mouth, the palm of your hands or in your mouth behind a condom).

Men will not communicate this fact as much, but the ultimate libido killer for him during a blow job is not just a bad blow-job (where technique was terrible) but to add insult to injury, the lover did not receive him in the end.

Equally, an awesome blow-job is reduced to a mediocre blow-job if the lover not only does not receive him, but rises up and off from his penis and begins to jerk him off while the penis head is exposed (rather than engulfed in your mouth bare mouth, engulfed in your mouth from behind a condom, or entrapped inside your hand).

## The Mental Versus Physical Aspect of Oral-Sex on Any Man

No matter what type of man he is: effeminate, average male or a manly-man; a man is at his strongest when someone is performing oral-sex on him. Regardless his socioeconomic status or any internal or external factors; *all* men are at their confidence peak when someone takes it upon themselves to take him in. The physiological, social, psychological, emotional, mental playing field is leveled for all men during oral-sex.

In performing oral-sex on a *woman*, there are so many positions in which you can have her-to heighten the experience-(because of the vulnerability behind the intimate moment and the fact that she is aware that she is being "taken.") When bringing the right kind of pleasure to a woman during oral-sex, she is weak and aroused-practically like a willing love-slave.

It's a different kind of "vulnerability" involved in an oral-sex intimate moment for a man. His only vulnerability is in the fact that you are "taking in" a sensitive part of him that carrying many physiological, social, psychological, mental strings. The "emotion" for him is the fact that he is being admired for that moment. Respect is being bestowed upon him by your willingness to take all of that in, for him.

With men, there is no need for positions in which to give him head to heighten the experience (so as to mind-fuck him while your mouth is-unlike you can do with a woman), because any "mind-fucking" that you need to do to him-you absolutely positively *have* to do while in the middle of giving him the blow-job. All "mind-fucking" moments are intertwined in: the way you give him head, your style, your technique, your ease, your rhythm and continuity, and how you handle his explosive moment when he ejaculates.

Through oral-sex, you are at his mercy while in the middle of that intimate moment-not him: you.

In his mind, you have submitted to him.

If done right, you have already mastered thorough pleasure for him, so there are only a couple ways to further add to this moment for him as well.

Unlike mind-fucking oral-sex positions that further weaken a woman; they make a man feel stronger.

The thing about performing oral-sex on a man is that no matter what position he is in-even if on his back-you are still taking *him* in and submitting to *him*, regardless.

If you are insecure or new at giving head, just keep him on his back to give him head-the next three pages of position examples would not be for you. But at any time you feel you are ready, secure and comfortable with giving head; here are some awesome position tips for you:

## Oral-sex Positions (for performing oral-sex on him)

There are some mentally intense ways to take him higher that will intensify the moment of oral-sex:

### *Kneeling in Front of Him*

This subservient oral-sex position is one of the top of the line positions you can be in to give him the full-effect of what oral-sex provides for a male. It's mental, and no different than what happens when someone kneels to you: they are in a permission to ask or beg something of you. It's a sexual mental power move for most men (especially the manly-man).

Obviously, while in this oral-sex position, you can pleasure his penis, and even better-his testicles (as elaborated on in #'s 1-9) however, you cannot get to his perineum while you are on your knees with him standing in front of you. In this position, you definitely want to keep your hands from being involved during the blow-job.

It's a better look to rest both hands on your thighs if you're sitting on the back of your legs. It's subservient-sexy.

If you are feeling cocky and you know you're about to give him one hell of a performance that he will never forget; give him the entire blow-job with your hands on your waist: super-hero-ish; or as if you are reprimanding him.

Make him feel your body language through your blow-job. Additionally, or at some point in the act, place your hands around his waist or hips while you are giving him the blow-job. Giving him head while you are holding his waist or hips is as if you are holding on to his face-giving him one good passionate kiss, yet the kiss is down below: his penis. It's a turn-on, too.

### *Against the Wall*

It's sexy for your back to be up against the wall while he stands in front of you to give him oral-sex. Because once his arousal is turned up, he will feel the need to grind you while your head is against the wall (especially if you are sitting on the back of your legs with your hands in your lap or sitting up on your legs). In this position, do not hold on to his waist or hips unless he gets too carried away with his grind. It can be exciting to subtly initiate a kind of "battle" between your mouth and his penis. It's exciting for him. In order for this "match" to take place-hold on to his waist or hips so as to let him know you are trying to take control. "Grind" (your face) into him with his penis deep into your mouth. That is the best way to make him feel that you are okay with his aggressive grinding. Take those deep aggressive pulls: repeatedly. Let him know that you are enjoying his grinding into you by nearly moaning a "yum" at each point that you open your mouth to devour, suck, and pull. This position plays on his nature, and once he feels that you are enjoying this aggressive grinding match-it will drive him up that wall that he is facing.

### Between Cleavage

If not from start to finish, while in the middle of a blow-job, it can be sexy for a man to take his penis and slide it between your breast-cleavage.

A lot of men are turned on by this however, it doesn't mean anything to have him merely slide his penis up down your two breasts (held together by you)-if at each time he is on the up-thrust, the head of his penis is not meeting your nice warm mouth; hungrily pulling and sucking on the entire head of his penis. It's mental. The turn-on about this technique is that if you are covering your breast nipples-it looks as though he is sliding his penis in to you from the rear. With your nipples covered, your breasts looks like an ass. This all plays with his thoughts. His senses are being played with in the fact that while entertaining the thought of the rear-entry visual, each time his up-thrust meets a nice firm suck and pull from your mouth, it interrupts the thought-with a pleasurable feeling to his penis that he is forced to savor.

Keep in mind that the more he can hear you actually sucking his penis as he pulls in and out of your mouth, the arousal gets higher for him. That is what makes him cum so hard during this technique.

## TIP 5 ~~~~~~~~~~~~~~~~~~~~~~~~~~~~~~~~~~~

### INTIMATE SEX and POSITIONS

Intimate sex and positions are like any other sex-position that you've probably been in before, however the receipt and delivery are different. In addition to that, some of what is being done in these positions *do* require courage and a slight release of our inhibitions (along with a partner who is willing to accept and enjoy the same).

Keep in mind that the concept of intimate *sex* is "consideration." Consideration for your lover and the intimate moment itself; getting to know their physical responses to the things you are doing to (and with them).

In order to gauge what that is, it requires that you "use your head" while having intimate sex. Take time to slow down the sexual act in order to really absorb your lover and allow them to absorb you, too.

Consider your intimate sexual positions as being more than physical, but rather: spiritual and mental, attached and steady. Not the kind of sex as if the two of you are on a on a timer; bodies pounding one another like you are trying to beat the other in obtaining that orgasm first.

All that is fine and good, for "fucking" and aggressive sex, but in the act of having intimate sex and in various positions; consider you human "dominion" over animals, for example:

Animals "fuck."

They do not take the time to stretch their mates out and love them from head to toe or take the time to create a sensual experience.

They mate, and they thrust, and they fuck. That is all.

They do not have the time to tailor their mating to the mate that they are with because they are animals-that's their nature, not ours.

We *do* have the capacity to do so but often times we just don't. Not necessarily because we don't want to, but because we tend to do things the way, and with the pace that they have always been done.

We are creatures of habit.

That is what this chapter tip is all about-nothing complicated and fancy; just the kind of sexual intimacy that requires a little bit of patience and pace; "tailoring" our lovemaking to the lover we are with by slowing it down and taking full advantage of the moment. By giving and being in receipt of the full effect of the sexual act and position itself (while in whatever position it may be) taking our time to show and slow our go.

Read on, so you can see just what I mean:

**Sixty-Nine**

The Sixty-Nine (69)-also referred to as the "twisted sixes," is an oral-sex position in which two people are performing oral-sex on one another simultaneously. Typically, the person with more body mass is on the bottom and the lesser is on top.

Couples also lie sideways to perform this sexual act (simultaneously) as well.

With regard to *intimacy*, this oral-sex position is least favorable (hence, why I did not list it in either of the "Oral-Sex for Him" or the "Oral-Sex for Her" chapter tips 3 and 4).

Good oral-sex has a premise: to please your partner and to give them your complete and undivided attention. The conclusion: climax.

You cannot give your partner your complete and utter undivided attention if you are being pleasured while at the same time-you are trying to give your partner pleasure. Somewhere, and at sometime in between this six-and this nine; someone is going to get preoccupied with their pleasure, or be so preoccupied with giving pleasure, that they are not in relaxed enough state to receive the pleasure they are being given.

This position is perfect for two people who are just "having sex," and have no interest or knowledge about the kind of true sexual intimacy (that I am teaching throughout this book). But for anyone who knows about the fine art of sexual intimacy; they know that the best oral-sex you can give to a lover starts first with giving him or her, your complete attention-uninterrupted-from start to finish.

The sixty-nine sexual position has nothing to do with true intimacy and the true willingness to thoroughly please your lover. A lover who is in-tuned with true intimacy and interested in giving their partner the full experience of oral-sex, would put their face right in their lovers crouch and get the job done (no matter how long it took), without their lover being bothered with having to touch in the interim and especially-simultaneously.

**Chair Ride**

It will forever be sexy and an intimate move to climb on top of your lover and straddle them before intercourse: fully-clothed, clothed just enough for your lover to have access to your crouch, and especially nude. The intimacy involved in this position comes from the fact that (unclothed or clothed) you and your lover are "public display of affection inappropriate," and the only thing between the both of you is your crouches. You being straddled atop your lover in this way will give them the freedom (and by you being in this position): the permission-to play with your body in a tightly closed area of exposure. The close proximity between the two of you is almost as if you are secretly at play. It's sexy. It's private.

Intercourse in this position is always sexy because of the position itself, but it's even sexier to expose your entire spiritual center to your lover in between the moments that you are straddled and riding during intercourse. Ask your lover to tell you things about you exposing yourself to them while the two of you intertwine in this moment. It turns up the fire and makes things hotter.

The key to this position being intimate and hot, is your ability to make full use of why you are sitting there. That being said; entice your lover into sharing the beauty of having you atop, facing, straddled, opened and exposed. The two of you will love it.

**Rear Entry**

The typical rear-entry/doggy-style sex position starts off a few minutes slow and going forward; ends up rough and rugged. There is a time and moment for aggressive sex (which we will touch on in the next chapter Tip 6), but here, it goes a little different when talking about *intimate* doggy-style sex position. When having *intimate sex*, in a doggy-styled position, the key to making the moment "intimate" versus "rough" is to allow your lover to bend you over far enough to where they can watch you from the rear while sliding inside you from the head to the very end of the penis.

Allow your lover to play this way, and watch the in and out with the head and the entire penis. That should be the focal point of this technique. Your moans of pleasure, the calm you have over your body and your willingness to allow your lover to take time to slide and out of you-and watch; creates this steady intimate moment. If you entice your lover into telling them to describe to you what they are doing, and that they love what they see; the intimate moment can last a good long while before the need arises to get raunchy and pounding begins. If you share this moment with your lover by letting them know that you are enjoying this, and enjoy listening to them tell you what is going on from behind; it will arouse your lover in ways that, I can assure you, throughout their day; that moment will not leave their frontal lobe. This method is good because you are teaching your lover to love your body and love what they are doing by watching it closely. It is extremely intimate (and unforgettable).

## On Stomach (cat style)

This position is sensual and intimate because you lay there flat on your stomach with either:

your hands stretched up and over your head, or clutched around a pillow; allowing your lover to have their way with you from behind. By your permission and merely lying there-not thrusting back, your lover has your full cooperation to play with and knead your buttocks and/or while burying themselves deep inside of your canal-nice and slow while grinding deeply. The only movement from you should be by way of your receiving this pleasure; your lover should never feel you move-only moan from the pleasure at each knead and deep grind. Notice I am saying "deep grind." Because for the sensuality and intimacy of the position to be created, the movement is not a "thrust," but rather, slow, deep and unforgiving grinds up and into you-the whole way through. This position can very well be torturous-in resisting the urge not to turn the grind into a thrust. If you feel your lover fighting to hard to resist the urge not to thrust; lift your bottom up just a little, to make them more comfortable. When you do that, your partner will sit up better on their knees so they can proceed grind you deeply. It's agonizing and explosive-but you both will love it.

## Corner Sex (on floor)

This techniques position is an awesome moment for sexual intimacy because you position yourself against the corner of a wall with your knees up and apart, allowing your lover to have full-view of you. The beauty of the act itself is that your lover can pleasure you with deep, slow grinds into you and there's nothing but a hard wall behind you to press into.

As with the previous position, the key to this is your lover resisting the urge to turn that grind into a thrust. With this kind of access to you, your lover is able to observe, and pull in and out then tease your genitals with the penis head or masturbate you.

This position can take you higher at the point when your lover grinds deep-upwards and into you for long periods of time before pulling out, as if they are trying to make you a part of that wall behind you. Your lover can pull out and observe you being open and exposed while you're in that vulnerable position; cornered such that you cannot move-just take all of it. Reaching climax in this position with those deep grinds into you is awesome and almost never ending, especially if your lover holds himself up and into you, and grinds you right.

**Side by Side**

This position is highly sensual (face-to-face) but best served on your side, and with your lover behind you. While your lover is inside of you from behind, they have access to your genitals-to masturbate you while inside of you. For you, this kind of pleasure is awesome. The other benefit of your lover being behind you while inside you is that they have the kind of access to you to pull you on top-with your back facing them. In this position, your lover is still able to masturbate you.

It's most sensual and most intimate to disallow you to

bounce or ride up and down-but rather, hold you firmly on top, as your lover grinds up and into you; while you to masturbate yourself.

As with the previous position, reaching climax in this position with your lover giving you those deep, unforgiving grinds up and into you is awesome and explosive-throughout (especially if your lover holds himself up and into you while pressing you down onto the penis).

It's a pleasurable kind of torture.

### On Top (rear-end facing partner)

This position is another one that you can share with your partner in bed, because as you are on top, and rather than a traditional ride/up and down thrust; what you would do is bend over and allow your lover to watch you handle the grind while they sit up some-watching themselves go in and out of you on top, straddled, with all your goodies in plain view.

It's even more exciting for your lover to get right there up and at you to hold you open, and watch themselves slowly go in and out of you: inch by inch, and all they can see is is the back of you-not your face.

It's very sensual and extremely intimate.

## Double-Chair Ride

Like the chair ride, but rather than facing your lover, what you would do is have your lover sit in the chair with you on top in a position to ride. You would have another chair in front of you [facing you-to support your arms and elbows] while you sit atop your lover with your back turned to them.

Like the previous position, the sensuality in this position is that your lover can't see your face but rather; your buttocks sitting in their lap. Unlike the previous position however (where your lover would have to sit up on their elbows in the bed) they would be in an upright position from sitting up in the chair, already. With you resting your elbows on the chair in front of you, this position takes a lot of pressure off your lover-and allows them to grip your bottom and use it like gears to control watching them go in and out of you. With the chair in front of you for support, this will allow you to move and wiggle your bottom about in ways that your lover can have a great time playing with-while watching themselves go in and out of you. This position is unbelievably awesome for your lover to watch in bright light. With them being positioned so comfortably in their own chair and you in yours, they can see every detail and movement of all the ins and outs while maneuvering you every which way. The most awesome part about this position is that your lover can proceed to take control by plopping you out of their lap and flat on to your own chair, propping your ass in the air and then hovering over *you* to ride *you* and grind you nicely, as if they are digging: deep.

It's unforgivably explosive.

**Edge of the Bed**

This position is highly erotic. It gives your lover a different angle to grind you to. It provides them the kind of access to you in which they can put their body mass into the deep grind, while supporting themselves by holding onto your bended knees with your legs open, or holding onto the back of your thighs while your legs are up. While at the edge of the bed, your lover can also turn you onto your stomach to grind into you from behind as well. Unlike lying down or sitting down while grinding deeply into you from other positions, in this position; your lover is on their feet. You are at the edge of the bed on your back with your legs open (or on your stomach with your legs wrapped around your lover) feeling the pressure of that slow deep grind which now has the power your lover's body mass behind it.

It is an agonizing and pleasurable experience that can make you climax octaves.

## Standing

Sexual intimacy in a (face-to-face) standing position is erotic and sexy in as much as the foreplay that is involved. As with the closeness of the chair ride, having your lover and you invade each other's space in this stance is intimate and sexy, alone. While standing, the feminine partner should be the one with the back against the wall. It is very sexy to have your lover caress your face, lips, neck, shoulders, and breasts while stretching your arms up to do so. Allow your arms to fall, for your lover to caress your neck and shoulders, and gently bite, lick and suck up and down the entire length of your arms.

Obviously, your lover can slide into you from the front, but (while in standing position) the best effect of intimate sex are given and received from the back. With your face against the wall, allow your lover to caress you all across and around the back of your neck and shoulders, back and arms.

Help prepare your lover to feel your arousal by taking the initiative to lean into the wall on the fronts of your arms and make your bottom erect for your lover to slide right into you. In this position, you are holding your body in such a way that your lover takes control and advantage of your entire bottom half. The key to this position is that your lover grabs you by the waist and gives you deep, slow and stiff grinds up and into you the whole way through. It is explosive. Take it.

## Missionary

This position is the classic feminine-masculine sexual position where the feminine spirit is the bottom lay and the masculine spirit is the top lay(er) and together they are: face-to-face, bodice-to-bodice, knee-to-knee, and foot-to-foot.

Awesome for the intimate sexual moment, because the position-itself, forces your lover to place their hands or arms one of three places: around your neck, around your arms (you-wrapped in theirs), or their hands in your hands. Perfect.

With your arms wrapped around your lover's neck and you guys positioned face-to-face, this missionary position gives you the opportunity to share intimate-passionate deep-kisses even in ways like the previous positions may not permit. Often times (in traditional sex) missionary position gets the bad name and is often joked about as being one of the most boring and basic positions to have sex in. But it's quite the contrary.

Missionary position has "magic."

One thing about missionary position is that if you can *really* "fuck," "make-love" *or* practice "intimate sex," you can do it in missionary position-period.

The more we get new illustrations in books about new

ways and new positions in which to have sex, we push the missionary position to the back-burner as if to do it, makes you a bad lover or boring in bed.

But what it *really* is-is that we have not taken the time out to realize that what the missionary position *really* is. It's too: personal.

The position requires a level of intimacy that a lot of us (merely having sex or "fucking") subconsciously know we shouldn't be doing. It's almost "secretly and subconsciously sacred."

Missionary is that *one* position that we would rather not entertain the thought of our lover cheating on us in. It is too "personal," yet, in general sex-related conversation "it's boring."

Allow me to play with your senses for a minute (where the missionary position is concerned).

Take a moment and image walking in on a cheating lover with their hands or arms either: around someone else's neck, that person's arms around your lover's arms, or your lover having them wrapped in their arms...Or how about your lover having that other person's hand in their hand, and together they are: face-to-face, bodice-to-bodice, knee-to-knee, foot-to-foot?

Low and behold, I'm willing to bet that if you had to

choose, you would much rather walk in on the two of them in doggy-style position rather than missionary.

If someone walked in on their lover cheating and the position they were caught in was missionary, you would probably argue your lover up and down that it looked like "love" rather than a "fuck."

We would instantly equate being caught cheating and fucking in doggy-style: the "fuck."

Yet, we are quick to call missionary position "basic" and boring.

That is because we *are* so busy "fucking" and "having sex" that we don't realize *just* how intimate it *really* is.

So with that being said, take advantage of this position, and the intimacy it offers. Share those deep passionate kisses, foreplay, and much needed conversations, apologies or expressions of love and appreciation you have for one another while being wrapped up in each other's arms.

Let that conversation build up the kind of excitement for the two of you that in between all those deep-kisses, caresses and foreplay; your lover holds you at your waist, forehead in your neck; and bring you nothing less than pure unadulterated hot passion with every generous, deep grind-up and into you until you can almost feel smoke coming from your ears.

## TIP 6 ～～～～～～～～～～～～～～～～～～～～～

**AGGRESSIVE SEX: WHY and HOW-TO**

By definition of what "intimate sex" is (as pertaining to this book's premise), there is nothing "intimate" about aggressive sex, but the fact still remains-we do have it.

As with any kind of sex-be it: intimate sex, the act of making love, fucking or aggressive sex; no matter the spiritual, mental or physical connection involved in either, in order for it to be *good* (aggressive sex), you still have to use your head.

Good aggressive sex is more than just a matter of fucking by way of bodies pounding together and trying to race to orgasm. Good aggressive fucking has to involve a mental and/or emotional element.

That being said, if you are going to do it, you have to make full use of the meaning of "aggression" and "fucking" as you would make full use of the moment, atmosphere and connection with your lover when having intimate sex (as elaborated in the previous "Intimate Sex and Positions" chapter Tip).

To fuck indeed means: "to have sexual intercourse with," but it also means: to treat unfairly or harshly, to meddle (*around* or *with*), to behave in a frivolous or meddlesome way.

Aggression is characterized by: unprovoked offensives, attacks, "invasions" or to make an all-out effort to win or succeed while in "competition" of sorts. And in this case: two bodies pounding against one another during [what really is] a selfish act of pleasure with another person under the guise of it being mutually shared, is a "competition" (of a sexual kind).

When you are "aggressive," you are vigorously energetic, pugnacious, forceful and assertive.

So to be *any* good at fucking, or aggressive sex, you have to take it a step beyond the act of two selfish bodies smacking against one another by two people breathing hard and/or moaning and shouting out from pleasure, pain, anticipation or all three.

As *spiritual divination* would have it: any time two human beings copulate for sexual intercourse, it is considered a spiritual act-regardless their emotional or mental attachment or commitment to one another, or not.

However, with regard to "intimate-sex" (by premise and definition of this book), consider the following:

## If you and your partner *ARE NOT* emotionally attached:

- Then the two of you are not involved in the intimate-spiritual act of sex. Therefore in good, aggressive fucking/sex; you two have to fully utilize the mental with the physical fact that you are merely pounding two bodies together as a means to an end.


- In this sexual situation (where you and your partner are simply fucking, and there is no mental or emotional attachment to one another) regardless if you are: in a sixty-nine position, a chair riding position, doggy-style, cat-style, on the floor in the corner, side-by-side, feminine on-top/rear-end facing partner, double-chair ride, edge of the bed, or standing position…the (*unspoken*) object of the act is for the less aggressive person to enjoy (and seek to be) treated like a slut during sex, and for the most-aggressive person to treat them as such.


  That is the mental + physical element of good aggressive sex/fucking (*between two people who are not* mentally and emotionally attached).

**If you and your partner *ARE* emotionally attached:**

- Then the two of you are involved in the intimate-spiritual act of sex. Therefore in good, aggressive fucking/sex; you two have to fully utilize the mental *and* emotional with the physical fact that you [still are] pounding two bodies together as a means to an end. That's just what "fucking" is about-regardless your commitment or emotional attachment.

- For the maximum (mental and emotional experience of a good fuck) antagonizing plays with the mind and emotions. During aggressive sex, this can be explosive (for the both of you). An example of such a thing is typically for the least aggressive partner to share secrets and "ghosts" of (a) lover/s past-where that other lover may have done something sexually, exceptionally well that the two of you never shared (in pillow talk conversation or ever), or perhaps you can bring up some redeeming sexual quality about another lover.
Human beings are like animals with regard to aggression. Animals use it to survive. Humans use it for fight or flight. While fucking, you are already in a hard-breathing almost animalistic state of sexual aggression, so, talk of anything to play on the mind and emotion of the most aggressive

partner will send them into sexual fight or flight. However, if your lover is far too sensitive for that kind of "play," then your other option is to somehow make them feel, not so much as "inadequate" about the fuck that they are giving you, but to force your aggressive lover to work harder at executing (whatever sexual position you are involved in at that moment) a little better or a little harder-so as to give them the impression that they are not pleasing you. This too, sends them into a sexual fight or flight mode.

- As well, in a sexual situation where you and your partner are emotionally attached, the object of the act is for the less aggressive party to enjoy (and seek to be) treated like a slut during sex, and for the most-aggressive party to treat them as such. However, it turns it up for the both of you if you *express it to one another* during the act, regardless the sexual position that the two of you are fucking in: chair riding, doggy-style, cat-style, on the floor in the corner, side-by-side, feminine on-top/rear-end facing partner, double-chair ride, edge of the bed, standing or missionary position.

That is the mental + emotional + physical element of good aggressive sex/fucking (*between two people who are* mentally and emotionally attached).

So, in addition the swift, pounding and selfish thrusts of trying to out-fuck one another and obtain that means to that "end," those are the ways you are supposed to "fuck" and have aggressive sex-if you want to do it *right*.

In rough/aggressive sex, it's not just about what you do or how you're doing it. It's also about what you do behind whatever it is that you are doing.

It's physical (sure).

But more than that: it's MENTAL-by all means…

### Doggy-Style and Aggressive Sex

Generally speaking, the sexual position itself is impersonal from its level of eye-contact (lack-thereof) all the way down to the position of the bodies involved in the act as well: merely pounding together (like literal dogs do) from the moment of insertion. There's no intimate methodology to it-other than your partner pounding you straight-in, pounding you towards the left, or pounding you towards the right.

If you and your partner are not emotionally attached, doggy-style is the optimum position to fuck in, because of its lack of physical contact and attachment to one another (aside from genital-to-genital). For these lovers with no emotional attachment or commitment; this position goes hand-in-hand like the missionary position goes over well on a wedding night.

But for the lovers who *are* emotionally attached and/or are committed, the "rear-entry" position (as elaborated on in the "Intimate Sex and Positions" chapter Tip 5), is the alternative to the typical detachment that this position has to "offer."

## Male Ejaculation

Male-ejaculation is a function that is designed to occur each and every time a male is involved in sexual activity of any kind, where it be: masturbation, oral-sex or intercourse; it has to happen (at climax). In the "Oral-sex tips for performing oral-sex on him" chapter Tip 4, we've already discussed how important a matter it is for the male to be "taken-in," and engulfed somehow, at ejaculation-whether it be: in your bare mouth, your mouth from behind a condom or entrapped in your hands. And in that section of the book, I did a thorough job in explaining how to do all three (for continuity in intimate sex).

The other (aggressive sex/fucking) option that a man has is better suited being done in an adult movie, rather than on your face (with regard to what "intimate sex" is, does, means and is about).

The message that this sexual act conveys, is atop the line in literal animalistic acts no different than a dog marking his spot with piss-yet the man is marking his spot with ejaculation onto a face.

With regard to the fine art of intimate sex, that kind of sexual activity has no place in it.

Intimate sex is about the instinctual, mental, and spiritual behind the emotion and/or physical act of sex. We, as humans do have animal instinct. But with regard to true intimate sex; ejaculation on the face is considered more "abnormal psychological-mental" rather than "(sensual)-mental" (as explained behind various sexual acts throughout this book with regard to the intimate sex).

Ejaculation on a face is better suited for entertainment purposes with regard to the fine art of intimate sex, as there is nothing: fine, intimate, or sexy about it. It is derogatory and degrading (where intimate sex is concerned). Period.

## *TIP 7* ~~~~~~~~~~~~~~~~~~~~~~~~~~~~

### THAT 21st CENTURY LOVIN'

That good, new-fashioned twenty-first century lovin': internet flirting, chatting/net-sex and text-sex.

If I have to admit so myself-it's extremely hot, alluring, mysterious, and sexy. It has just that hint of unexplainable mystery about it that even I can't resist having a taste of, from time to time.

I grow and evolve with the change in times, unchain my wireless heart if you can. I'm just a 21st century kind of girl: A Girl in the World and the World in a Girl, and I plead the 5th.

We are living in a stage of the information-age where now, most of how we socialize and take care of business is online or by way of our hi-tech phones. Our cell phones aren't even built for talking anymore-have you noticed that?

We're almost annoyed to talk on our cell phones nowadays.

They're just not ergonomically friendly to us the way they once were.

We can't even hold them the way we used to and we don't even converse and turn our cell phones much anymore, because they've lost all their curves.

Our cell phones seem to be more compatible with our fingers than our ears. It's like our fingers are having a love-affair with our phone's qwerty keys and our computer's keyboard; boo'ing and woo'ing one another back and forth behind pixilated words and images.

Cyber space is this mysterious world we have become accustomed to, and made ourselves comfortable with. The ambiance and anonymity of sitting behind pixels with nothing but what we pick and choose to reveal of ourselves, is a kind of power afforded all of us on a leveled playing field (so we think). But the "power" actually lies behind the energy-itself.

Our pixels and words create a spirit of some kind: a kinetic or cryptic energy of sorts.

This "power" is the literal unspoken.

What we literally have not heard.

What we literally have not seen.

Our perception (for most), intuition (for some) and "sixth sense" (for others) are getting a massive workout-night and day.

While utilizing the conveniences that all of the gadgetry and gratification that the 21st century has to offer us; it is still important to not to lose touch with and become desensitized to our natural way of communicating and relating one another.

Voyeuring the lives of other people is the norm, nowadays.

All things that were once sacred and secret are now sensational and salient.

As we watch in real-time: "real-life" kind of entertainment; more and more we become desensitized to "real emotion." When they cry, we merely observe (rarely do we cry with them) however, we are entertained by it. Slowly but surely the most emotion we are beginning to understand is that which we feel no authentic connection to, unless we *are* "entertained" by it.

We sit in the cyber sphere recognizing the only emotion as that which comes across the rolling screen IN CAPS!!!!AND EXCLAMATION POINTS!!!!-sitting in the peace and serenity of our private dwellings running away with assumptions and drawing conclusions on things and people whose hand we never shook, whose eyes we never looked.

The truth is, we're not "getting any." Getting anything we can sink our teeth into for any amount of time *as compared* to the 21st century socialization and our love-affair with it.

In comparison to the way we are keeping up with the

times, the tangible ways that we once related and socialized are losing in the game of intimacy.

So it's important to remember that while we can't help but socialize and communicate in ways that are current with the time, nothing can replace a true intimate connection with another human being.

But we can however, have a little fun doing it. And sometimes...it is necessary.

## Phone Sex

Phone sex is so underestimated and often times the butt of many jokes in conversation. But don't underestimate the power of phone-sex. It is the ultimate safe-sex tool and could save your heart, your emotions and your time.

Phone sex (like the internet and all its emotional flirting and sub-flirting affairs) still allows your prospective partner the choice not to have to get all dolled or suited up for you, if they just don't feel like being all that impressive for the moment. It's an awesome, occasional technique to use with our lovers when we are distant from one another and we've already been sexually intimate, however-essential when courting or dating someone who we may become sexually intimate with, at some point.

In courting someone, phone sex is not a "promissory note." Treat it like a liaison between you and your prospective partner. Let it be the bridge over what could save you from (possible) troubled waters, later. It can help you dodge a lot of bullets and can rescue you from being notches under countless belts, a world of regrets the next day (or after the act-going forward). So look at it as being the opposite-equivalent of the morning after pill. With it (phone sex) you can gauge whether or not there should even be a night-before deal.

Phone sex is a definite guarantee that you will have gathered all that you need to know about a person's sexual style, and that will help you gauge whether or not that person is sexually for you, or no.

Let's be realistic, sex is a major necessity in a relationship or sexual connection and everybody doesn't like the same thing. Why wait to find in-position and mid-moment?

If you (and your prospective partner) are comfortable enough to have phone sex, chances are, you already know what you're working with and if you'll work-together.

If you are comfortable enough to initiate phone sex, you definitely know what you are working with and are serious about love-making and who you'll do it with. Any prospective sexual partner will have gathered this much about you, and if they know or learn nothing else about you, if anything-they should respect you for it, should you go forward (sexually), or not.

Additionally, phone sex is a good indicator of your prospective partners level of passion, their desire for you

you, if anything-they should respect you for it, should you go forward (sexually), or not.

Additionally, phone sex is a good indicator of your prospective partners level of passion, their desire for you (*outside the bedroom*), and what, if any, inhibitions or hang-ups they have about all things sex.

Sensual lovers are (typically) more willing to please you. Through phone sex, you can find this out about your lover. Any kinks or quirks that you like, don't like, are willing to accept or are not willing to accept, can be uncovered during phone sex.

Granted, unlike net/chat sex and sexting; phone sex can be a little more intimidating because you are allowing your prospective partner to hear your every moan and tone.

Let it happen naturally-don't force it. While doing so, let your inhibitions run free and communicate the things that most turn you on about the act of and during sex. With enough of that kind of flow going back and forth-you will know if you are sexually compatible with that person.

Take into consideration that the actual physical moment with another person can bring about things unexpected and unplanned, but when it comes to knowing what you like during sex, you can get your questions answered beforehand, during that phone-sex conversation. That way-all else in the moment of the actual physical connection should be total gifts and bonuses.

Phone sex is most often enjoyed by people who are masturbators and the little less-inhibited.

Net/chat sex and sexting are the other alternatives, so let's talk about that:

## Net Sex/Chatting

Chatting can be alluring, fun, sexy, and sensual because you are behind pixels on a screen and your partner (prospective or mysterious) is behind another.

It's a little less "personal" than phone sex because you don't have to deal with the vulnerability of allowing that other person to hear your voice respond or initiate.

Through net sex/chatting, your partner has to read every line that you type in order to sense your arousal- by way of the words that you type.

In comparison to phone sex, this technique would allow you to gather the same information that you need to know about your prospective partner, however you are most likely to get more of the prospective partners "truth" via chatting, because they do not have the worry of your voice on the phone responding to (or not responding to) whatever it is that they are typing.

I would choose this option over phone sex (initially), because it is not so evasive and "in-your-face" or "in-your-ear." It gives you or your prospective partner time to work each other slowly.

If this option is available to you, I would suggest it (first) before phone sex. It still affords you the anonymity that you may need, while still assisting you in gathering whatever intimate information you need from the prospective partner to make a decision (or not) to go further; while at the same time, enables you to let your inhibitions run free.

Being able to hide behind pixels to communicate (whether about sex or simply getting to know another person), can be tricky. Because while at the same time a person is able to hide behind the pixels and allow their inhibitions to run free, they *could* also hide behind it and lie, fabricate or exaggerate about things up to and including what they can, will and won't do. The best way you can deal with that is to know that people lie about the things they wish were true. How you wish to handle that would have to totally be up to you, and your individual situation.

That is where phone sex returns to steal the torch back from this net/chat sex tip.

Not to say that the same can't be true for phone sex, but you are more apt to get the truth about what a person can, will and won't do when they are able to hear your voice and gauge your responses to whatever they say-versus sitting there in the quiet and reading your replies on a screen.

That is the reason why so much miscommunication happens on these forums and such, because you cannot see or hear whatever it is you are trying to express in words out into the cyber sphere-in mere quiet. All feeling of emotions like: empathy, sincerity, etc. are not as easily communicated in words by all people. By the same token all emotions aren't received and understood by all people as well. In the cyber sphere, if whatever you say isn't accompanied by exclamation points or caps, for some people's eyes (on the receiving end of the pixels); you nearly have to be a poet in order to express whatever it is you are trying to say or convey.

So, in trying to get to know one another: sexually, intimately or otherwise, it would be a good idea to begin net sex/chatting. But eventually, it should be followed by stepping it up to the phone, even if not for phone sex; by phone-nonetheless.


## Text Sex/Sexting

An awesome tool for couples who have surpassed that "getting to know you" stage, and wish to use it for those spontaneous moments in the day when one, or the other person feels the urge; sexting (otherwise) is the bottom of the barrel of recommended options for "distant" intimate moments. That is because it is far more impersonal than net sex and chatting, and a far cry from the intimacy of actual phone sex, and because the sexting method can be done while on the move, for that reason, I would not recommend it. 21st century methods of connecting to the prospective (lover, partner or significant other) are only as useful as it allows you an immobile kind of privacy, and in creating anything intimate-ambiance is key.

Although connecting with one another while on the run is possible, with regard to intimacy-this method is an epic fail, because intimacy involves commandeering and isolating the senses. That cannot be done while mobile and moving about. The (personal) attention required is divided.

With phone-sex, chances are, both parties are most probably lying there tucked away in some part of a dwelling while on the phone-hands in pants-or caressing other parts of their bodies; absorbing the words communicated in each other's ears and enjoying the sound of one another's voice.

With net-sex/chatting, chances are, both parties are sitting there most probably in the privacy of some dwelling while on their laptop or PC; absorbing the words electronically communicated and put in front of each other's eyes-for the imagination to create the pictures with in order to tantalize the senses.

Whereas with text-sex/sexting, you have no way of knowing whether or not you are getting the undivided attention of your partner. If you are in anyway serious about the intimacy involved with getting to know your partner, I would not advise using this method.

Part of the usefulness in taking advantage of some of this 21st century lovin' is that it is an *alternate* (or temporary) form of intimacy.

I do take in to consideration that different people have different emotional and physical needs and desires.

There *are* people who receive complete satisfaction in connecting this way for years on end. For them, phone sex, net-sex, chatting and text-sex/sexting *is* "intimacy" enough for them. (The psychology behind that does not fit the concept of this book-so I'll stop there).

In the greater scheme of things, with regard to our 21st century options in intimacy: phone sex, net-sex, chatting, and sexting are equally as (physically) "safe" as abstinence is for the physical body. So, that is something to consider.

Now, consider this:

# TIP 8 〜〜〜〜〜〜〜〜〜〜〜〜〜〜〜〜〜〜〜

## USING SEXUAL PROTECTION

Sexual protection can be intimate and fun, while integrated as a part of oral-sex and intimate sex-position techniques.

Ideally, we'd all like to put our complete trust in our lover, partner, or significant other (with regard to having natural free-flowing oral-sex and sex), but the fact of the matter is-we can't be so sure.

The idea of this chapter is not to turn this book into a knock-down drag-safe sex education read; but rather-offer some safe-sex options to "match" some of the sexual situations as discussed in:

chapter Tip 3-Oral-sex (for her)

chapter Tip 4-Oral-sex (for him)

chapter Tip 5-Intimate Sex and Positions

chapter Tip 6-Aggressive Sex: Why and How-To

## Dental Dams
## (For oral-sex on a woman or rimming/salad tossing on her or his anal opening)

A dental dam is a rubber rectangular sheet of latex that is used in dentistry however, as times have progressed, we found additional usage for them. It's no longer a secret. Now that it is known that dental dams can serve as a method of prevention of sexually transmitted diseases, the traditional dental dam is now sold in different colors and flavors and marketed as a dam for "pleasure."

With a dam, you can perform oral-sex on a woman or anal rimming on a man or woman with the dam covering actual flesh (the vaginal or anal opening) so that the lover can still give the same pleasure, but with a layer of protection for their own mouth. Although it can be a tedious extra step that takes away from the naturalness of female oral-sex or anal rimming; the other benefit of its use (while performing oral-sex on a woman) is that (unlike without the use of a dental damn); her lover can apply a significant amount of sucking pressure to her clitoris that she otherwise, could not.

Additionally, (for those women who like aggressive play on their clitoris'), with the use of the dam, their lover can pleasure them with gentle nibbles and pulls of the clitoris with their teeth from behind the dam-which too, can be an explosive feeling when that orgasm is reached.

For optimal pleasure, before placing the dam on top of the

vagina, you might want to apply a lubricant specifically designed for sexual activity, so as to make it "slippery" enough for the dam to glide over the clitoris to give off the feeling of having a warm wet mouth on it. All the while, you are playing from *behind it* with your mouth. Though it can be tedious and a bit messy (trying to keep it in place) if used properly; the dam will protect you from possible sexually transmitted diseases while you still get the job done for her.

The "slippery" feel will provide her with the feeling of having a warm, wet mouth performing oral-sex on her- although you will be behind the dam, doing so.

As far as dams being used for anal rimming (for him or for her-just the same), it is what it does: covers the anus opening and allows the lover to provide anal rimming pleasure without contracting possible sexually-transmitted diseases or bacteria from the anus.

As with the dam's use for vaginal oral-sex, a lubricant can be applied at the anal opening-so as to make it "slippery" just enough for the dam to slide into the anus with the lovers strong tongue providing pleasure from behind it.

The thing about pleasuring an anus, whether female (and especially male); with or without a dam, the anus is pleasure-sensitive to the deep stroke and swift tongue-action going in and out of it and in various directions- anyways, so, don't disregard the dam.

## Flavored Condoms vs. Regular Condoms (For male oral-sex)

Providing oral-sex to a male with a condom can be intimate and fun, too.

Often times, it is not enjoyable to the giver because of the choice in condom they are using: a traditional lubricated latex condom that is made specifically for anal or sexually intercourse. They do not taste very well and are often times packaged with a lubricant that does not taste very well either (on top of the taste of the latex itself). That would easily turn one away from using a condom while giving head to a man. But there are other options out there. There are flavored condoms on the market-which come in a wide variety of colors and flavors. Additionally, these condoms do not have the powdery consistency that some regular condoms can have on them, nor or are they packaged with lubricants that leave an awful taste in your mouth.

Giving head with a condom on can really be pleasurable for both parties. The fact of the matter is this: if you are *really* skilled in giving good head; you can do it with a condom on-definitely.

The trick to making sure your male partner can get as close the experience of getting head without a condom is to apply a significant amount of lubricant on his penis and stroke it as if you were jerking him off.

Next, place the (flavored) condom over his penis.

That gives him "insulation," to prepare him for the pleasure you are about to give him (from behind that condom). Don't leave the man high and dry. Don't put a dry condom on top of a man's penis and expect him to get an experience as close to having a warm, wet mouth on it. Men typically do not enjoy receiving head from behind a condom for that very reason, as well. By applying lubrication on his penis before you put the condom on it will, followed by proceeding to give him an awesome blow-job as I showed you (see #'s 1-15 in the "Oral-Sex for Him" chapter Tip 4), your man should barely remember that he had a condom on.

Additionally, the other plus to giving head with the condom on (that without-is a definite "no-no" in giving a good blow-job and as explained in #5/"Oral-Sex for Him") is that you can get your teeth involved. On top of a condom, using your teeth to tease and glide up and down the shaft and the mushroom head of his penis is awesome for him.

The plus *and* bonus of giving head with a condom on is that you can give your man that ultimate experience that he is already looking for at the end of his blow-job: the pleasure of being able to cum in your mouth. With the condom on-he will still get that lovin' feeling however, you will be protected from any possible sexually-transmitted diseases.

Truth be told, you can give him twice the pleasure (while

protecting yourself in the interim).

Don't count the condom out.

It has more power-play than often taught or talked about, although I would argue that it does have some room for improvement.

How so, you ask?

Well, as I made mention in the "Oral-Sex for Him" chapter Tip 4: "*A man also knows that his penis holds a kind of "power" as well. I would jokingly add that if it didn't, how or why is it massively manufactured and duplicated the world over, impressively more anatomically correct and precise than any anatomically correct" vagina has ever been manufactured?*"

To that, after your having just read how messy the use of the dental dam can be while trying to perform oral-sex on a woman (in comparison to the options available for oral-sex on a man) I might also add: "*...because we will forever have a ways to go-to find that perfectly snug condom for protection of performing oral-sex on a woman, if ever at all.*"

# ~ABOUT the AUTHOR~

Angela Sherice is a writer and expressionist of: erotic, self-efficacious, introspective, reflective and metaphysical fiction and non-fiction books.

Get acquainted with her by visiting: **www.angelasherice.com**

There, you can read her bio, connect with her via her online communities, read her blog, synopsis' & excerpts of her other books (as pictured on the next page over), as well as find the sale locations where all her works are sold.

INGEST.  FEEL EMPOWERED.  BE ENLIGHTENED. GET INSPIRED.

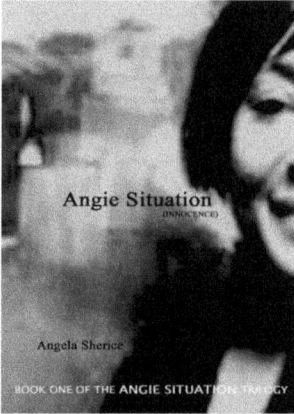

*Prequel*

**Angie Situation (\*INNOCENCE)**
**ISBN: 978 09709806 63**
Fiction  biographical / Drama

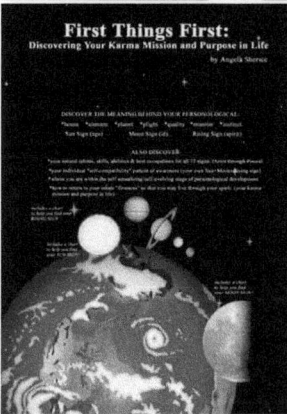

**First Things First:**
**Discovering Your Karma**
**Mission And  Purpose in Life**
**ISBN: 978 09709806 32**

Astrology | New Age| Personal
Success | New Thought|
Spirituality | Metaphysics

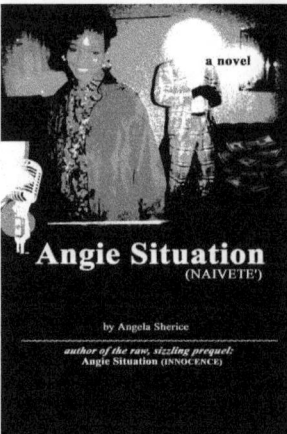

*Sequel*

**Angie Situation (NAIVETE' )**
**ISBN: 978 09709806 56**

Fiction  biographical / Drama

CXXX

# Doing It!

*Mind-Blowing Sex Tips You Will Never Forget*

*(The Fine Art of Intimate Sex)*

*by* **Angela Sherice**

KARMAIC PUBLISHING